$100

50
Trail Runs
in
Southern
California

50
Trail Runs
in
Southern
California

STAN SWARTZ
JIM WOLFF
SAMIR SHAHIN, M.D.

THE
MOUNTAINEERS

Published by
The Mountaineers
1001 SW Klickitat Way, Suite 201
Seattle, WA 98134

Published simultaneously in Great Britain by Cordee, 3a DeMontfort Street, Leicester, England, LE1 7HD

Manufactured in the United States of America

Project Editor: Dottie Martin
Editor: Brenda Pittsley
Cover and book design by Kristy L. Welch
Layout by Kristy L. Welch
Maps by Ben Pease
All photographs by Samir Shahin, M.D., unless noted otherwise
Trail elevation profiles by Jim Wolff

Cover photograph by Brad Wrobleski/Masterfile
Frontispiece by Anthony Nex

Library of Congress Cataloging-in-Publication Data
Swartz, Stan, 1934-
   50 trail runs in Southern California / Stan Swartz, James W. Wolff, Jr., Samir Shahin.
      p.   cm.
Includes bibliographical references and index.
   ISBN 0-89886-700-2 (pbk. : alk. paper)
   1. Jogging—California, Southern—Guidebooks. 2. Running—California, Southern—Guidebooks. 3. Trails—California, Southern—Guidebooks. I. Title: Fifty trail runs in Southern California. II. Wolff, James W. III. Shahin, Samir. IV. Title.
   GV1061.22.C2 S92 2000
   917.94'910454--dc21

                                                        00-008164
                                                          CIP

To Naimma Shahin for her constant love, support, and inspiration.

And in cherished memory of Sattar Shahin.

To the loving and fond memory of Albert and Marian Swartz.

To Jim and Geraldine Wolff for their love and guidance.

CONTENTS

Trail to Inspiration Point, Santa Barbara

SAN GABRIEL MOUNTAINS
Los Angeles, Pasadena, Claremont, Rancho Cucamonga

JOSHUA TREE NATIONAL MONUMENT
Twentynine Palms, Palm Springs

ORANGE AND SAN DIEGO COUNTIES
Laguna Beach, Irvine, Santa Ana, Anaheim, San Diego, El Cajon, Escondido

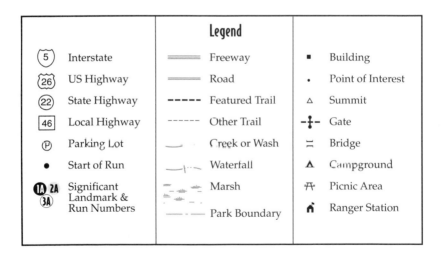

Legend

(5)	Interstate	≡ Freeway	■	Building
(26)	US Highway	≡ Road	•	Point of Interest
(22)	State Highway	----- Featured Trail	△	Summit
46	Local Highway	------ Other Trail	-•-	Gate
Ⓟ	Parking Lot	⌣ Creek or Wash	=	Bridge
•	Start of Run	Waterfall	▲	Campground
1A 2A 3A	Significant Landmark & Run Numbers	Marsh	开	Picnic Area
		Park Boundary	⋔	Ranger Station

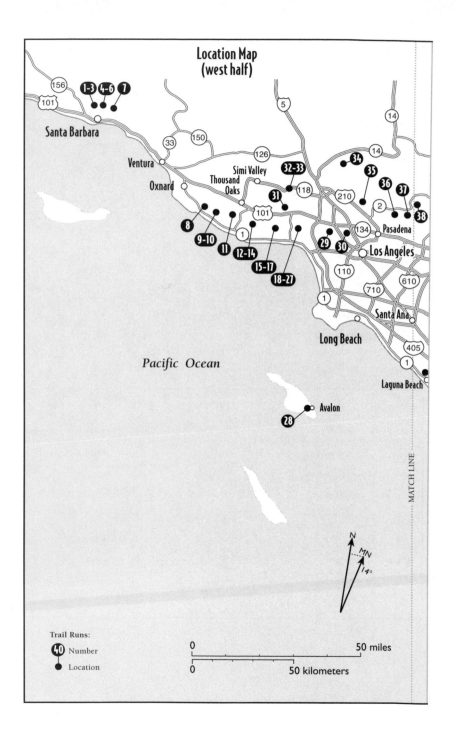

Location Map
(west half)

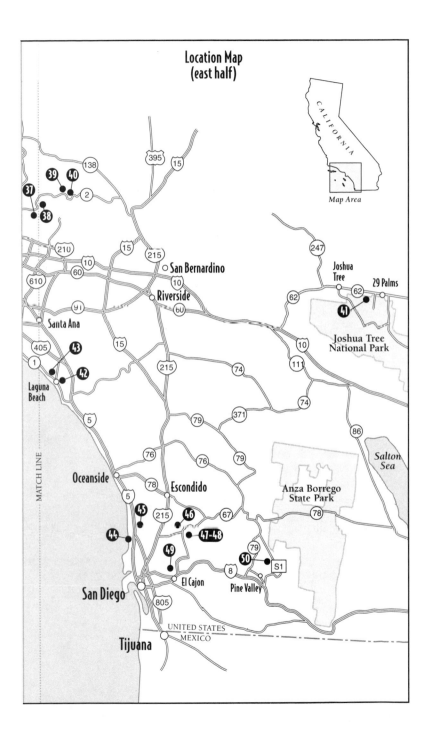

Location Map
(east half)

CALIFORNIA

Map Area

FOREWORD

I have always been an athlete. I believe I came into the world already working out. Anything that kept me outdoors was a part of my life: swinging from trees, riding, dancing, running, swimming, and just about anything else you can think of.

I have been a triathlete for most of my professional athletic career, but the core of my athletic soul comes from running. It is the activity I stay close to, the one I turn to when I need to regenerate and recharge. Trail running is the ultimate form of this sport. It gives me what I need most to challenge my spirit and get in touch with what I believe is the essence of life: nature.

I have personally run, raced, and explored a great many of the trails in Southern California. Nothing beats the thrill of discovering a new trail and making it one of "my" runs.

More than any other form of locomotion, running takes me to places I never would see otherwise. Although the solitude and serenity of running the trails make me feel like the world is mine, these trails are there for all of us to enjoy and find a little part of ourselves. This book is long overdue for all the "athletes" who share the passion of trail running. As the arena of off-road activities continues to grow from simple trail running to orienteering, adventure racing, and the like, this book will be the gem that every outdoor enthusiast will want to have.

I may have started my running on the urban roads of South Africa, but I see nothing but the trails of Southern California in my future.

Paula Newby-Fraser
Eight-Time Ironman Triathlon World Champion and
author of *Paula Newby-Fraser's Peak Fitness for Women*

Spring foliage in La Jolla Valley, Santa Monica Mountains

ACKNOWLEDGMENTS

The invaluable support and generosity of many people contributed to helping us write this book. First, we thank Elaine Swartz, Leona Wolff, and Debbie Bradford for their love, patience, understanding, and support during the many hours spent working on this project.

We are grateful to fellow Trail Runners Club members for their active participation. Willy Blumhoff, Amy Chan, Zhanna Drantyev, Irving Hoffman, Kirsten King, Andrea Moore, Catherine Spears, Paul Spencer, and Bridgett Walsh participated in many exciting runs and photo shoots and have kindly allowed us to use their images.

Cheryl Anderson and Chad Derum both took time off from work to help us. Cheryl traveled to San Diego and Santa Barbara, where her energy running up the big climbs was greatly appreciated. Chad was our guide on the Franklin Canyon run and accompanied us to Joshua Tree, donating his water bottle to a very special cause on the bumpy flight back home in Samir's plane.

We acknowledge Nancy Spear with great appreciation for her editing expertise. Thanks to Julie Degraw for her wonderful attitude and faithful assistance with transportation on several trips to San Diego. Matt Kavanaugh, Harold Simon, and John Wood provided helpful legal and publishing advice. Anthony Nex captured many visual images with his remarkable photographic skills. It would have been difficult to complete this book without their combined help.

Ron Webster deserves our thanks for his devoted trail building efforts in the Santa Monica Mountains. Those trails have contributed measurably to the growing sport of trail running. Nancy Hobbs, executive director of the All American Trail Running Association (AATRA), was instrumental in encouraging us to author this book. Finally, thanks go to each trail management agency that provided clarifying comments about the great trails we love to run.

Narrow trail in Santa Monica Mountains

INTRODUCTION

50 Trail Runs in Southern California is for the increasing number of runners who want to combine the beauty of nature with the physical challenge of trail running. Southern California has some of the best mountain and desert trails anywhere, and excellent weather conditions make the region ideal for trail running. These trails are only a short drive from the major cities of Santa Barbara, Los Angeles, and San Diego.

The authors have a combined total of forty-five years of running experience. We want to share our love of trail running with you and help you enjoy its many physical and mental benefits. This guide aims to introduce both beginning and experienced runners to the many wonderful sights, sounds, and smells waiting to be discovered through trail running.

How to Use This Book

These courses require the usual attention to traffic, road and trail conditions, weather, terrain, the capabilities of your party, and other factors. Because many of the trails venture across lands that are subject to development or change of ownership, conditions may change, rendering use of some routes impractical. Keep informed on current conditions, obey private property signs, and avoid confrontations with property owners or managers. Exercising common sense is the key to a safe, enjoyable outing.

All runners regardless of experience should read the Trail Running chapter. It is a great refresher for frequent users and a good introduction for novices. Trail veterans should at least read the parts on health and safety to refresh their training on these important topics.

Trail descriptions are organized in five groups according to geographic areas or mountain ranges. Trails are listed in order from one end of a geographic area to the other and each has a map and a trail profile. Directions for getting to the trailhead and staying on course are explained along with a quick-reference summary.

To begin, select an area of interest and review the trail profiles, descriptions, and list of trails in the appendix to find trails that fit your ability and needs. Studying the landmarks and terrain associated with each trail will enhance your enjoyment of the run and should keep you from getting lost.

Fire road at east end of La Jolla Valley, Santa Monica Mountains

Catalina Island

There are four course configurations: out and back, point to point, loop, and out-and-back loop combinations. Out-and-back, out-and-back loop, and loop runs require only one car. Point-to-point runs require two cars, one to leave at the finish and one to take you to the start. Many point-to-point runs can be converted to out-and-back runs by running all or a portion of the course and then turning around. This can be done from either end of the course. Each course description provides all the information you need for planning transportation.

Each run has been assigned a difficulty rating based on distance, steepness, elevation, and altitude. The ratings are easy, moderate, and strenuous. Use the ratings as a guide and weigh them against your individual experience and ability.

The minimum and maximum estimates of the time it takes to run each course are based on a calculation of 8 and 15 minutes per mile and then adjusted slightly based on our experience running these courses.

Why Run on Trails?

It is a crisp morning; dew turns to fog and floats gently above the ground. Birds and rabbits rustle in the brush. The hillsides and canyons glow as the sun rises. You run swiftly along the soft terrain and enjoy your surroundings stopping occasionally to enjoy the magnificent views of the surrounding mountains. In the cool canyons, you cross gurgling streams protected under a lush canopy of trees.

This is a typical trail running experience.

What is so special about running on trails? Trail running is a delightful way to get away from it all. Many of us live in big cities with their attendant comforts and annoyances. Running on trails provides a welcome opportunity to leave this hectic environment and enjoy nature. The peaceful settings free you from distractions and allow you to think more clearly. Traveling up hills and down canyons, a runner is transported both physically and mentally. Everyday concerns fade away—the next well-planted step is all that matters.

Trail running is a grand adventure. You experience the extremes of heat and cold. You encounter the wilderness and its perpetual changes caused by fire, erosion, landslides, and fallen trees. You see seasonal fluctuations firsthand: the colorful wildflowers of spring, the filling and drying out of streams, the grasses turning brown in the sun, the leaves turning from green to red and falling off the branches. Regular visits over the year allow you to enjoy these processes.

Because you are away from motor vehicles, the air is cleaner and there are no inhibiting traffic lights. Coyotes, deer, rabbits, fox, squirrels, snakes, frogs, and birds are common on the trails. Viewing wild animals in their natural environment is always a special experience.

Running exclusively in urban settings typically limits you to predictable hard, smooth surfaces. Trails, meanwhile, are softer and more forgiving than concrete and asphalt and spare your body from undue wear and tear. This benefit is especially obvious on longer runs. Many runners report much less soreness after running long distances on trails versus running even shorter distances on pavement. This may be because the softer and more varied surfaces distribute the work across all the leg muscles and because trail running generally forces a slower pace.

Further, trails have challenging obstacles such as tree roots, rocks, boulders, low-hanging branches, blind turns, steps, ruts, mud, stream crossings, overgrown weeds, poison oak, wildlife, and steep hills. All present challenges and the irregular surfaces strengthen additional muscle groups and firm up tendons, ultimately making you less prone to injury.

Elfin Forest in San Diego

Running on trails rather than city streets also causes less mental fatigue because you concentrate more on your surroundings and private thoughts and less on the act of running and the traffic.

TRAIL RUNNING

You can lose your breath quickly when running up steep hills. Your muscles may be unused to this effort and your heart will race as you pant for air. Trail running develops your fitness in ways that flat roads cannot.

Your ability to climb and descend hills will develop quickly. The key is to go slow and avoid getting so short of breath that you have to stop. Run within yourself, moving forward at a steady and deliberate pace. It is okay to walk up the steeper hills. Keep in mind that although you may be running slower than usual, your effort level is the same as or greater than running faster on a flat course.

Lean slightly forward and use your arms to help propel you when running up hills. Shorten your stride and try running more on the balls of your feet rather than on the heels. These subtle changes will improve your ability to move smoothly and efficiently up steep slopes. Soon, you will breeze up inclines with new strength. When you return to flat courses, your improvement will amaze you and your friends.

Training

Trail running is demanding. It requires you to run up and down hills with many abrupt turns while at the same time negotiating uneven surfaces and avoiding obstacles. This requires strength, stamina, balance, vision, and coordination. Do not expect to maintain your usual pace when running hills. Accept the fact that you will go slower. Keep your arms, chest, shoulders, back, and neck relaxed to make respiration easier. Avoid becoming short of breath while running uphill.

Begin adding distance and speed slowly. Advancing too quickly is the leading cause of injury for beginning trail runners. Start on relatively flat trails or rolling (not steep) hills, and combine running with walking. Increase your mileage in increments and remember that there is nothing wrong with walking uphill or downhill on steep or rugged terrain. Even the most experienced trail runners will walk on steep terrain.

Trail running does not normally lend itself to speed because the uneven terrain makes it difficult to go fast. Speed can increase with experience, however. Be sure you are sufficiently warmed up before running fast. Begin cautiously on the wider and relatively smooth fire roads to avoid tripping on uneven surfaces.

Trail running as compared to urban running strengthens different muscles in the feet, ankles, legs, back, abdomen, and upper body. Ankle tendons are conditioned on the trail's irregular surfaces and abrupt turns. Calves, hamstrings, and quadriceps are strengthened from running up and down hills, and the abdomen and upper body develop tone from the twisting and turning required for balance.

Improving your body strength and flexibility will increase your trail running ability. Cross-training exercises like mountain biking, swimming, strength training, yoga, racquet sports, and stair climbing are excellent for this purpose. A balance of strength and flexibility will lead to more efficient running and fewer injuries.

Trails and Fire Roads

There are several types of trails, but their common characteristic is that they are unpaved. Fire roads can accommodate motor vehicles. It is easier to run on fire roads because they are wider and smoother than narrow trails.

Narrow trails usually accommodate individual runners in single file. Narrow trails are more varied and interesting and generally more isolated than fire roads. Many narrow trails prohibit cyclists.

Multiple-use trails can accommodate pedestrians (hikers and runners), cyclists (mountain bikes), and equestrians (horses and riders). Multiple-use trails are wider than narrow trails and have additional vertical clearance to accommodate riders on horses or bikes. Be attentive when you are on a multiple-use trail so you can anticipate approaching pedestrians, equestrians, or cyclists. Often you will hear others approaching before they hear or see you. If you hear a cyclist coming, move to the side of the trail to avoid a collision, regardless of who has the right-of-way. If a horse and rider are approaching, it is wise to slow to a walk or stop altogether until they pass to avoid startling the horse.

As a further caution, remember that running in the rain can damage delicate trails and is not recommended. Stay on larger fire roads when possible if conditions get wet.

Clothing and Gear

The sport of trail running requires special clothing and gear to keep you comfortable over a range of distances, weather, and terrain. Shorter runs require less support gear than longer ones. Most of the runs described in this book will keep you out on the trail for 1 to 4 hours. You need to carry everything required for comfort and safety. Basic clothing includes shoes, socks, shorts, shirt, and a hat. Cooler weather may require gloves, tights, windbreaker, long-

Fire road above Avalon, Catalina

sleeved shirt, and a warm hat. Additional gear for longer distance running includes a fanny pack to carry food, water bottles, first-aid supplies, and personal care items, such as lip balm, sunscreen, and tissues.

Shoes: "What kind of shoes should I wear?" is probably the most frequently asked question by those new to trail running. The best shoe is one that fits well and is comfortable. Costly trail running shoes are not necessary. You will do fine with regular street running shoes. Later, you may want to try shoes designed specifically for trails. These shoes typically provide better traction, support, durability, and protection than street running shoes. They are also heavier and have a different feel that may not be agreeable to everyone.

Properly fitted shoes are important for your running enjoyment. It is a good idea to visit a running store that has a knowledgeable staff who are also runners. These experts will evaluate your specific needs for motion control, stability, and cushioning. They can help you find shoes that are compatible with the motion and shape of your foot. When you try on different shoes, be sure to wear the same socks and orthotics you will use when running. Buy shoes later in the day when your foot is larger. Do not be surprised if the recommended running shoe is a full size larger than your street shoes. Never buy a shoe that is too small thinking that it will stretch; it won't. Ill-fitting shoes can cause painful blisters and black toenails.

Socks: Socks cushion the foot to prevent friction against the internal surface of the shoe and provide a moisture control system that wicks moisture away. Some socks provide additional protection against the specific effects of cold and rain. Experimentation is the best way to discover which socks you like best. Some runners prefer inexpensive socks for trail running—they just throw them away after the run instead of picking out burrs and struggling to remove dirt stains. Some prefer 100-percent cotton, while others prefer socks made of synthetic fibers.

Moderately padded crew socks (covering to just above the ankle) made of a synthetic fabric designed to wick moisture away from the foot are a common choice. Taller socks provide more protection against low-growing vegetation and prevent dirt and rocks from entering at the top. Loose and wrinkled socks can cause blisters. A good skin lubricant will help prevent blisters and chafing.

Insoles and Orthopedic Inserts: Many runners replace the original insoles supplied by the shoe manufacturer with thicker ones that provide extra cushioning. These insoles have extra padding on the heel, ball, or arch of the foot. Many runners wear prescribed orthopedic inserts, sometimes in combination with insoles bought off the shelf. As with socks, always bring these insoles and inserts to the shoe store when trying on new running shoes. This ensures that new shoes fit properly before you purchase them.

Gaiters: These garments have elastic cuffs that fit over your socks and the top of your shoe to prevent rocks and dirt from getting inside. You might consider buying a pair if you run on gravelly trails and wear low-top shoes. However, the propensity for accumulating dirt or stones inside shoes or socks is often a function of an individual runner's stride as much as the style of sock and shoes he or she wears.

Hats: Hats keep the sun off your head and shield your eyes from glare. They help keep you warm in cool weather and prevent sweat from running down your face and into your eyes. Always wear a hat on longer runs in the sun. The legionnaire style is ideal for sun protection. It has a generous bill, an absorbent sweatband, a removable neck drape, and a chin strap for use in windy conditions. Some hats are made of materials specifically designed to block UVA and UVB rays.

Most body heat escapes from your head in cold weather. An appropriate warm hat is made of wool or synthetic fleece that wicks moisture away from the skin. Some hats have flaps to lower over the ears for extra warmth.

La Jolla Valley Trail in Santa Monica Mountains (Photo by Anthony Nex)

Sunglasses: Sunglasses protect your eyes from the harmful effects of the sun and from windblown dust and debris. Glasses should be lightweight, comfortable, shatterproof, and have a wraparound design that provides 100-percent UVA and UVB protection. An elastic band that attaches to the ear pieces and fits snugly around the back of your head will keep glasses from bouncing and slipping down your nose.

With or without sunglasses, runners should approach shadowed areas cautiously to avoid accidents caused because their eyes did not have time to adjust to the suddenly dim light—you can trip during the split-second period of temporary blindness. Sunglasses make it even darker. Removing sunglasses in shady areas will help you see obstacles. Those who rely on prescription glasses can consider flip-up clip-on sunglasses for fast removal.

Sun Protection: Do not ignore the harmful effects of sunlight. Protect yourself by wearing a hat and applying sunscreen to exposed skin. A wet-from-sweat white cotton T-shirt has an SPF 4 rating, which is not enough. Those with fair complexions, light-colored hair, and light-colored eyes should consider clothing designed to provide protection of at least SPF 15. Hats, sunglasses, shirts, shorts, pants, and even gloves are available with SPF protection.

Always use sunscreen when running outdoors. We recommend that you carry extra sunscreen lotion in your car. Remember, it is important to use sunscreen even if the weather is cloudy. Saving time by skipping a sunscreen application is a bad idea. After a couple of hours in the sun, when you are getting tired and dehydrated, a mild sunburn will consume valuable body fluid and can increase your chances of fatigue, heat exhaustion, or even sunstroke. Use a sunscreen that blocks both UVA and UVB rays with a minimum rating of SPF 15 or preferably SPF 30. Sunscreens that are waterproof or labeled 8-hour will not easily sweat off and can protect you throughout a long run without reapplication. Sunscreens often sweat off your forehead and tend to burn and irritate your eyes. To avoid this problem, apply sunscreen on the face only below the eyes; your sunglasses and hat will provide protection above the eyes.

Rain Gear: If weather conditions change, running in heavy rain and cold temperatures for long periods can be miserable without a good jacket. It also puts you at risk for hypothermia. A good quality jacket appropriate for the expected conditions allows you to enjoy a run in inclement weather. Lightweight windbreakers offer minimal protection against moisture. More expensive, sophisticated jackets are constructed with different shells and liners that breathe, allowing sweat to wick out while preventing rain from getting in.

Finally, plan ahead and know that having dry clothes waiting in your car at the end of the run is a welcome comfort.

First-Aid Kit: On longer runs in remote areas, it is wise to bring along some basic first-aid articles. Minimal supplies stored in a waterproof bag might include antiseptic pads, bandages, antibiotic ointment, wash-and-dry pads, moleskin, ibuprofen (or other pain medication), 2-inch tape, lip moisturizer, an athletic bandage, and a small tube of anti-chafing lubricant. Use the water in your bottle to irrigate debris from eyes and to moisten a cloth to clean scrapes.

Map and Compass: Runners on an unfamiliar course can become disoriented and uncertain of their whereabouts when there are few landmarks or if the sun becomes obscured. A map and compass help you stay oriented. Small, inexpensive compasses that fit around your wrist or slip over your watchband are available in sporting goods stores. Keep a map in your pack for ready access.

The top of most maps is north. Align the indicator on the compass to north (zero degrees), and then align the map so that the north side is perpendicular with the compass indicator. The map is now positioned correctly relative to the surrounding topography. If you are unfamiliar with how to use a compass and map, ask a friend or a staff person at your local sporting goods store for help. Take a little time to learn the basics.

On longer backcountry runs (not necessarily those covered in this book), you might consider using an electronic Global Positioning Satellite (GPS) instrument. These lightweight instruments indicate longitude, latitude, direction, and altitude from any location on earth. Such a tool could prove invaluable on some unfamiliar trails.

Venom Extractor Kit: Rattlesnake bites are unlikely but possible in Southern California. Inexpensive, lightweight venom extractor kits are available in many sporting goods stores. A venom extractor pump employs a syringe-style vacuum system that removes venom when used promptly. The small, rubber suction cups found in old-style kits do not provide enough suction to be of much benefit. Follow the detailed instructions that come with these kits. Preventing and treating rattlesnake bites is detailed in the First Aid and Safety section later in this chapter.

Gear and Fluid Carriers: There are several types of carriers to choose from for packing your gear and water. A step up from individual, hand-carried bottles are waist belts with pockets for gear and straps that hold one or more water bottles. Larger bladder systems fit around the waist or on your back, feature pockets for gear, and supply water through a hose that allows you to drink at any time. Sport drinks can be carried in bottles, but only water is recommended for bladders because of the difficulty with cleaning them. Choose a system that is comfortable and large enough to carry all the water and gear you will need on any given run.

A small pack will suffice on shorter runs, whereas a larger pack is necessary for longer runs. Many trail runners own two or three different packs to accommodate a wide range of conditions and distances.

Additional Suggestions: Tuck an extra car key in your pack for emergencies. The frustrating mistake of locking yourself out of your car can spoil the fun. Bring identification with you. For wilderness runs, carry a small flashlight and matches. Leave word with friends or relatives regarding where you are going and for how long. Ask people you meet in remote areas for information about conditions on trails that they have visited recently.

Hydration and Nutrition

Every runner knows the importance of hydration before, during, and after running. Start drinking plenty of water days before a long run and carry plenty of fluids during the run.

How much water should you carry? The average runner should drink 5 to 12 ounces of fluid for every 15 minutes of running. This adds up to 40 to 96 ounces of fluid over a 2-hour period (long enough to cover 10 to 12 miles). Most bottles hold approximately 30 ounces. Bladder systems hold between 60 and 110 ounces or more. Always try to carry enough water for the run and a little extra. If you are well hydrated at the beginning of a 2-hour run, two water bottles should be adequate at moderate temperatures and elevations.

Carry extra water in case you need to rinse scrapes, flush debris from the eyes, or assist someone in need. In addition, you may unexpectedly find yourself spending extra time on the course. Keep in mind that your water usage will increase when it gets hot and at higher elevations. The course descriptions in this book note whether water is available on the trail. Sometimes these water stops may be inoperable or have been removed, so do not rely on them exclusively.

In addition to drinking several glasses of water 20 minutes before starting, enjoy a small breakfast before a morning run. Sometimes dashing out the door with a sport bottle in one hand and a banana in the other is adequate. A banana provides about 60 calories and leaves the stomach in about 30 minutes. If you plan to run for less than 2 hours, you might get away without eating anything. Nevertheless, hunger may catch up with you toward the end of the run and you'll wind up going slower.

Runners on urban roads are often close to markets with food and beverages, but trail runners must carry their supplies with them. There are many tasty and lightweight high-energy foods, such as sports bars or energy gels, designed for the endurance athlete. Be sure to carry some of these on longer runs. Bread, fruit, cookies, and sandwiches are also terrific fuel and will never taste better.

Experiment to determine what foods work best for you. Having a little extra on hand can come in handy if you are out longer than expected. Share extra portions with other runners who find themselves low on energy near the end of a long run.

Weather, Temperature, and Altitude

Southern California is generally warm and sunny, but rain, wind, and altitude can combine to produce extreme conditions at each end of the spectrum. Always get up-to-date weather reports before starting out, and pay attention to flash flood warnings. If you have any questions or concerns about the conditions in an area where you plan to run, call a nearby ranger station or the local agency responsible for that area. Contact numbers are listed in the appendix.

To protect yourself during cold spells, dress in layers. The multiple layers will keep you warm, and you can peel them off as the temperature rises. Watch for hypothermia symptoms toward the end of a wet run. Recognizing and treating hypothermia is detailed in the First Aid and Safety section later in this chapter. Muddy conditions increase the risk of slipping and falling, so use extra caution and slow down or walk to prevent a painful fall on rock-strewn trails.

Iron Mountain Summit Trail in San Diego

At higher altitudes, a runner must be aware of snow, ice, and lower oxygen levels. If you are used to running at sea level, you will tire faster and run slower at higher elevations. The trails described in this book are no higher than 7,000 feet. Although altitude sickness does not normally occur below 10,000 feet, some people will experience headaches. Carry some ibuprofen or aspirin, just in case. If you have limited experience running or hiking at higher altitudes, start slowly.

A hot day should encourage early morning starts. High winds can cause low visibility because of dust in the air; difficulty with balance on steep, tricky trails; and windburn, so avoid running along exposed ridges in those conditions.

First Aid and Safety

Safety is an important issue in any outdoor activity. No guidebook can alert you to every hazard or anticipate the limitations of every reader. Running alone in the mountains, especially in unfamiliar territory, is not always advisable. Use judgment and common sense and know your limitations.

Trail running can take you far away from medical help. Most trail environments are not hostile or dangerous, but it is important to be aware of certain potential nuisances. Common first-aid issues on the trails include sprains, falls, foreign bodies in the eye, and poison oak exposure. Tick infestation, snakebites, and encounters with mountain lions can occur. Basic first-aid knowledge allows you to treat these injuries with confidence. The Mountaineers recommends that you always carry the following Ten Essentials on any backcountry excursion: extra clothing, extra food, sunglasses, knife, firestarter, first-aid kit, matches in a waterproof container, flashlight, map, and compass.

Falls: Anyone can be caught off guard and trip, especially going downhill when following someone too closely. When falling, it is instinctive to place your hands in front of you, resulting in scrapes on the hands and knees. After a spill, remain calm and collect yourself before getting up. Irrigate any scrapes with water while you gently massage them to clean out any ground-in dirt. If you have petrolatum, you can apply some to the wounds as a protective barrier.

Strained knees and twisted ankles may force you to slow down or walk. If a sprain is not too severe, you can often shake it off and keep going, but do not force yourself if you are in pain. If you have tape in your pack, you can wrap your ankle or knee to make a good support brace.

Eye Irritations: Dirt or pollen can get in your eyes. The safest immediate remedy is to use water from your bottle to irrigate the eye. Avoid rubbing as you may embed any particles deeper into the eye tissue.

Poison Oak: Poison oak primarily grows in semi-shaded areas near water. Usually, it is seen as a bush or vine standing 2 to 3 feet high. It can climb up tall plants, however, and is sometimes encountered at head and shoulder levels. Frequently used and well-maintained trails are usually wide enough to avoid poison oak. Learn to recognize its three-leaf configuration and stay clear of it.

Poison oak deposits resin on the clothes and skin. Avoid touching affected areas to prevent further exposure. If possible, wash off the resin with soap and water within 15 minutes after exposure. Some running trails pass near restrooms where this is possible. After you get home, do not handle the contaminated clothing, and wash it separately from your other clothes. Apply cold, wet compresses to blisters, keeping them on for 20 minutes and applying them five times a day for a few days to control blistering and severe itching.

Cool tub baths are a soothing antidote for a poison oak rash. You can add colloidal oatmeal to the water to control widespread inflammation. Calamine lotion also helps a bit. Antihistamines, such as *hydroxyzine* and *diphenhydramine*, control itching and may help you sleep (25 to 50 mg every 4 hours is the recommended dosage). Skin lotions containing camphor, menthol, and aloe also help provide relief from itching. Topical over-the-counter products are available for use before and after exposure to help prevent the effects of poison oak. Topical steroids such as cortisone cream will help reduce the itching but will not penetrate blisters. In severe cases, your doctor can prescribe stronger steroid creams and oral *prednisone*.

Hypothermia: Hypothermia results when the body cannot generate enough heat to maintain normal body temperature. This is brought on by exposure to cold conditions over a period of time. All runners are susceptible to hypothermia if cold or wet weather blows up unexpectedly. Symptoms of hypothermia include uncontrolled shivering, slow or slurred speech, fumbling hands, stumbling and loss of coordination, drowsiness, and exhaustion. Hypothermia is a life-threatening condition; take corrective measures immediately.

If these symptoms occur, find a dry shelter to avoid more exposure to the cold, rain, and wind. The following may not be immediately available, but if you are near help, do the following: Get into dry clothes and drink warm, nonalcoholic liquids such as tea, bullion, or even hot water. Get near a fire or other heat source to warm up. If you are assisting a victim who has serious hypothermia, remove both your clothes and the victim's clothes and climb into a sleeping bag together to encourage skin-to-skin heat transfer between you and the victim. Keep the victim awake and give encouragement.

Do not continue on the trail run even when a victim seems to have recovered. The main thing is to avoid getting cold and wet. Dress in layers with a good outer shell. Keep your hands covered with gloves, and wear good socks and a warm hat.

Ticks: Should a tick adopt you as a host, it will attach itself in a protected spot on your body. If you notice a slight irritation, check it out immediately as ticks should be removed promptly. It takes an hour or more for a tick to burrow in, so it can be removed easily if you find it in time. Check yourself thoroughly after every run and again when you are back home and ready to step into the shower.

Avoid removing ticks by direct finger contact. It is best to use tweezers or a thread, but if you have no other choice, shield fingers with a rubber glove or cloth. Using tweezers, grasp the tick as close to your skin surface as possible and pull upward with steady pressure, and continue with light, steady traction for a few minutes. Out on the trail, you can use a loose thread from your clothing. Make a loop and pull it over the tick at the tick's narrowest body part. Pull both ends hard enough to lift the skin. The tick will slowly back out after a few minutes of upward pressure. Avoid squeezing the tick. If possible, disinfect the bite area.

The use of petroleum jelly, fingernail polish, isopropyl alcohol, or a hot match are poor methods for detaching ticks because they do not work well and may cause the tick to regurgitate body fluids. Do not twist the tick during extraction as this increases the possibility of its mouthpart detaching and remaining embedded in your skin.

The possibility of contracting Lyme disease in Southern California is small; however, if a fever, headache, rash, or muscle aches develop after you have been in a tick-infested area, you should see your doctor for a diagnosis. Blood tests do not detect Lyme disease until 10 days after the illness develops.

Rattlesnakes: Rattlesnakes have wide, triangular heads, two facial pits, and vertical pupils, and many, but not all, will sound a warning rattle when disturbed. They are most active between March and October and when temperatures are between sixty-five and ninety degrees Fahrenheit. Rattlesnakes do venture out at night, so if you are running after dark, fire roads may be safer because they provide better visibility than trails.

Snakes are not interested in you unless you invade or threaten their space. To avoid doing this, watch where you step and be very careful where you put your hands. If you do encounter one, give it a wide berth. If you hear the rattle, stop and locate the source of the sound. Move away slowly so that you do

Dramatic rock formations in Santa Monica Mountains

not trip and fall. If your momentum will not allow you to stop, you might have to jump over or around the snake—do your best to avoid this, however. If the snake remains on the trail and prevents your passage, stay away from it and stomp on the ground. The vibration usually will encourage it to slither away. Be patient and give it a few minutes to pass.

Field treatment of a rattlesnake bite begins with staying calm. Many rattlesnake bites are dry (no venom injected) and only rarely are they fatal. Do not risk a second bite by chasing after the snake or trying to capture it. Immobilize the injured body part below the level of the heart. All rings, watches and constrictive clothing should be removed. The victim should be reassured, placed in a resting position, kept warm, and taken to a medical facility as quickly as possible. The victim should not be allowed to walk if it can be avoided. A venom extractor pump is of greatest benefit when used within the first 5 minutes after the bite and kept in place for 30 minutes. Do not use ice, tourniquets, or incisions.

Mountain Lions: It used to be extremely rare to see a mountain lion (also called cougars), but sightings and close encounters are reported more and more often as human development encroaches on their territory. These big cats are primarily nocturnal and avoid contact with humans. If you are confronted by a mountain lion, it is recommended that you stand up tall, wave your arms, and make yourself look as big as possible. Yell and fight back if attacked.

Maintain close supervision over young children who may accompany you. If a mountain lion appears, pick the children up and put them on your shoulders. Avoid crouching, because to the mountain lion you may appear to be prey. Unlike other animal attacks, fighting back is often successful with mountain lions.

Solo Travel: Some trail runners enjoy running alone or simply do not have a partner. Solo runners should still tell someone where they are going and should be more compulsive about bringing along extra supplies. Cell phones are useful accessories for solo runners to carry in their packs (many mountain peaks provide excellent reception).

At the same time, a runner in a group is safer and learns more quickly. You are more vulnerable to the elements and wildlife when running by yourself than when running with friends. For these reasons, you should consider joining a trail running group.

When running with others, stay at least 6 to 8 feet apart to allow adequate visibility. Always run single file on narrow trails.

Getting Lost: If you think you're lost, admit it first to yourself and then to others in your group. Confirm your last known position and return to it, or remain on a well-traveled trail and wait for help. Most of the trails in this book are not far from civilization, and there is a fair amount of foot traffic, so be patient. Usually within an hour a cyclist or hiker will come by and help guide you. When a trail seems to fizzle out, or the trail is not going where you expected, slow down and assess what happened. The best way to prevent getting lost is proper preparation. Having a general idea of what to expect and where you are going will give you the big picture and increase your confidence.

Trail Etiquette

Ask a trail runner what is special about running on trails and you'll probably hear about being out in nature, how quiet and serene it is, or about the joy of getting away from the noise and pollution. These reasons all have a general theme, a respect for nature and our relationship with it. Southern Californians are very fortunate to have so many varied and gorgeous trails. Trail runners tend to be wonderful and caring people. We are proud of our resources and we enjoy sharing them with others. That pride must extend to every runner who ventures onto a trail. That means pack out your trash! Do not bring pollution in with you. Stay on marked trails and leave no trace.

You are encouraged to keep the noise down to preserve the peaceful surroundings usually found on trails. Runs often start early in the morning and you may be parking your car and getting ready near a sleeping residential neighborhood. People who meditate, paint, or write also use the trails to pursue their interests. Respect the tranquillity found in our vast wonderland.

Extend general courtesy to everyone you meet along the trail. A simple nod of acknowledgment to a passerby is fine. When you are approaching someone

Ray Miller Trail (Photo by Anthony Nex)

from behind and you intend to pass, always call out "on your left." This lets them know you are there and indicates on which side you will be passing. When running with several people, it is a good idea to let oncoming traffic know how many runners are behind you. A quick "three more behind" tells someone to continue cautiously. Regulations require cyclists to yield to runners and equestrians, and runners to yield to equestrians. Regardless of these regulations, always yield if there is any doubt about your safety or the safety of others.

Trailhead Parking

Most trailheads have parking lots; some are free and some charge a small fee. Parking also may be available on nearby side streets. Always obey posted parking restrictions or risk having your car towed or ticketed.

An Adventure Pass is required to park in Angeles, San Bernardino, Los Padres, and Cleveland National Forests. You can purchase an Adventure Pass for $5 per day or $30 per year at ranger stations and sporting goods stores.

A Note About Safety

Safety is an important concern in all outdoor activities. No guidebook can alert you to every hazard or anticipate the limitations of every reader. Therefore, the descriptions of roads, trails, routes, and natural features in this book are not representations that a particular place or excursion will be safe for your party. When you follow any of the routes described in this book, you assume responsibility for your own safety. Under normal conditions, such excursions require the usual attention to traffic, road and trail conditions, weather, terrain, the capabilities of your party, and other factors. Because many of the lands in this book are subject to development and/or change of ownership, conditions may have changed since this book was written that make your use of some of these routes unwise. Always check for current conditions, obey posted private property signs, and avoid confrontations with property owners or managers. Keeping informed on current conditions and exercising common sense are the keys to a safe, enjoyable outing.

The Mountaineers

SANTA YNEZ MOUNTAINS
Santa Barbara, Ventura, Oxnard

These beautiful, rugged mountains rise steeply above the city of Santa Barbara like a giant wave about to crash. They separate Santa Barbara from the Santa Ynez Valley, making travel between these areas difficult in earlier times. They are part of a series of transverse mountain ranges in Southern California and rise more than 4,000 feet just a few miles from the sparkling Pacific Ocean.

There are many wonderful trails to explore just a short distance from downtown Santa Barbara and nearby Monticeto. Following these trails through riparian woodlands and along boulder-filled streams, through sage scrub and chaparral hillsides, and under groves of pines, sycamores, and oaks is the best way to enjoy the natural settings.

The courses have excellent views of the ocean, surrounding mountains, and distant valleys. The hillsides are steep and there is no water available. Know your limits and carry a lot of water, especially in hot weather. You will find trail running in the Santa Ynez Mountains a real treat.

Jesusita Trail

Distance: 8 miles
Course geometry: Out and back
Running time: 1.3–2.3 hours
Start altitude: 500 feet
Finish altitude: 500 feet
Elevation gain: 2,400 feet
Highest altitude: 1,830 feet
Difficulty: Strenuous
Water: None
Area management: Pueblo Lands of Santa Barbara
    Los Padres National Forest
Maps: Santa Barbara (USGS)
    Los Padres National Forest (Forest Service)

This course traverses lush canyons with stream crossings and switchbacks up the mountainside. Rustic ranch houses in a meadow remind you of the area's rich historical background.

GETTING THERE

From Oxnard or Ventura, head west on Highway 101 and get off at the Los Positas exit. Turn right toward the mountains. After crossing State Street, Los Positas turns into San Roque Road. Continue straight ahead. Park just beyond the Cater Filtration Plant on the left.

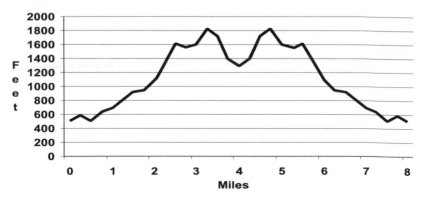

THE RUN

The trailhead (1A) is located just north of this parking area on the west side of the road. Head north on the well-maintained dirt road that is part of the Jesusita Trail. There are stream crossings as you travel into the canyon (1B).

At 1.25 miles the trail joins a dirt road (1C) where you will see a bridge off to the left. Continue straight ahead to the north on the dirt road and at 200 feet turn right on the intersecting fire road (1D). After 200 yards, note a smaller dirt road joining sharply from the right (1E) so that you will avoid it on the return trip. Go through the steel gate and continue northeast uphill.

Jesusita Trail

After 100 yards there is a bulletin board on the left; continue a short way on the road. Immediately after crossing the stream, take the small trail going to the left (1F).

Continue 3.25 miles and a smaller trail will begin on the right paralleling the road (1G). Take the smaller trail, which soon turns left, crosses the road, and then passes under power lines. There is a major stream crossing (1H) as you cross to the east side of the canyon. The huge boulders in the stream are worth contemplating. The trail joins a larger fire road (1I) 0.15 mile after the river crossing. Continue downhill for 200 yards on this wide fire road and you will see the Tunnel Trail (1J) on the left marked with a sign. This is the turnaround point; return to the start the way you came.

Option: Continue up the Tunnel Trail until you get to a ridge near power lines. There are expansive views of the Pacific Ocean and Santa Barbara from this vista. Return to the start the way you came.

SIGNIFICANT TRAIL LANDMARKS

1A. Trailhead north of parking area on west side of road.
1B. Stream crossings.
1C. Trail joins a dirt road. Continue straight ahead to the northwest for 200 feet.

1D. Intersection with fire road. Turn right and pass through the steel gate. Continue in a northeasterly direction.

1E. Pass road intersecting from the right.

1F. At the bulletin board, continue on the road and immediately after crossing a stream, take the trail to the left.

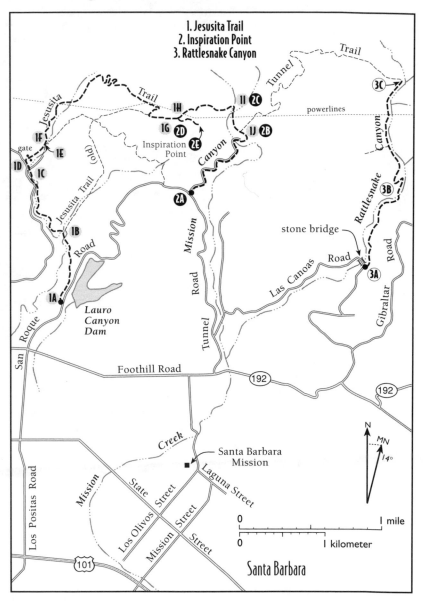

1G. After 3.25 miles, take the smaller trail that begins to the right of the road. The trail turns left, crosses the road, and goes under power lines.

1H. Stream crossing to east side of canyon.

1I. Trail joins a wide fire road. Continue downhill 200 yards to a sign on the left identifying the Tunnel Trail.

1J. Intersection with the Tunnel Trail. This is the turnaround point. Return to the start the way you came.

Inspiration Point

Distance: 3.6 miles
Course geometry: Out and back
Running time: 0.5–1 hour
Start altitude: 950 feet
Finish altitude: 950 feet
Elevation gain: 1,200 feet
Highest altitude: 1,800 feet
Difficulty: Strenuous
Water: None
Area management: Pueblo Lands of Santa Barbara
    Los Padres National Forest
Maps: Santa Barbara (USGS)

This short but challenging run provides excellent views of Santa Barbara, the foothills, and higher mountain peaks. The first 0.75 mile is on a paved road up the hillside. Lush vegetation lines the rest of the trail and there is a

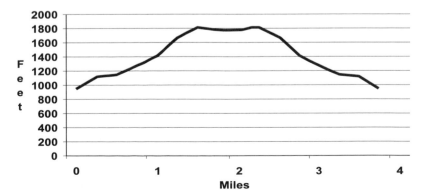

Inspiration Point in Santa Barbara

stream crossing amid huge boulders in a dramatic, steep-walled canyon. After your run, consider a visit to the nearby Santa Barbara Mission, Museum of Natural History, and Botanic Gardens.

GETTING THERE

From Highway 101 in Santa Barbara, exit at Mission Street and drive northeast toward the mountains. This becomes Mission Canyon Road as you pass the Santa Barbara Mission. Continue north to Foothill Road and turn right. Shortly, at the fire station, turn left on Mission Canyon Road and keep to the left at the first intersection where Mission Canyon Road turns into Tunnel Road. Drive to the end of Tunnel Road and park nearby.

THE RUN

Follow the paved road (2A) behind the gate uphill and over a bridge into the canyon. Shortly after crossing the bridge at mile 0.75, the paved road ends, marking the beginning of the Jesusita Trail (2B) on the left. The Tunnel Trail is on the right. Continue north up the canyon on the Jesusita Trail. As you head up the canyon, cross the stream (2C) and then begin the climb out of the canyon on a series of short switchbacks. The trail winds through sage scrub and chaparral and is moderately steep in places.

The trail ends at a wide fire road (2D) at the top of an intermediate ridge high above Santa Barbara. Pick up the trail directly across the fire road to the left. This narrow trail parallels the fire road and provides excellent views of the city and foothills below. This area is known as Inspiration Point (2E). On clear days, you can see more than 50 miles of coastline, making it worth your effort to get here. The trail will eventually rejoin the fire road, which is a good place to turn around and return to the start on the same course.

SIGNIFICANT TRAIL LANDMARKS
2A. Trailhead is paved road behind gate.
2B. Paved road ends, marking beginning of Jesusita Trail. Tunnel Trail intersects from the right.
2C. Stream crossing.
2D. Trail ends at fire road. Cross fire road and turn left onto trail to Inspiration Point.
2E. Inspiration Point. Continue on trail to fire road. Return to the start the way you came.

3
Rattlesnake Canyon

Distance: 3.5 miles
Course geometry: Out and back
Running time: 0.5–1 hour
Start altitude: 940 feet
Finish altitude: 940 feet
Elevation gain: 1,050 feet
Highest altitude: 1,880 feet
Difficulty: Moderate
Water: None
Area management: Pueblo Lands of Santa Barbara
Maps: Santa Barbara (USGS)

This moderately difficult course follows a boulder-lined creek in a canyon with forests of sycamore and oak trees. The lower section of the trail is well shaded with many waterfalls, pools, and grottos. There are several stream crossings and a series of switchbacks on the way up to an expansive coastal view. The name is fearsome, but the risk of encountering a snake is no different here

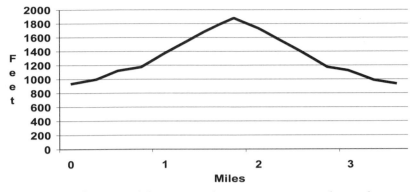

than in any other beautiful canyon in this mountain range. The combination of wooded trails along a stream and unbeatable views is sure to make this course one of your favorites.

GETTING THERE

From Highway 101 in Santa Barbara, exit at Mission Street and drive north toward the mountains. This becomes Mission Canyon Road as you pass the Santa Barbara Mission. Continue north to Foothill Road and turn right. Drive 0.02 mile and turn left on Mission Canyon Road at the fire station. Drive 0.5 mile and make a sharp right turn on Las Conoas Road. Drive 1.2 miles and park right after crossing the stone bridge. The trailhead is just to the right (east) of the creek.

THE RUN

Run north from the trailhead (3A), which is 75 yards east of the stream. There is a stream crossing at 0.75 mile (3B). You will catch glimpses of waterfalls and quiet pools, as well as vistas of the foothills and the coast. Follow the main trail as you encounter additional stream crossings. The intersection with the east end of the Tunnel Trail (3C) is the turnaround point; return to the start the way you came.

Option: For additional mileage, continue as far as desired on either one of the connecting trails at location 1C and return to the start the way you came.

SIGNIFICANT LANDMARKS

3A. Trailhead is 75 yards east of stream. Run north.

3B. Continue north at stream crossing.

3C. Intersection with the Tunnel Trail. Return to the start the way you came.

Rattlesnake Canyon

4
West Cold Springs Trail

Distance: 3.5 miles
Course geometry: Out and back
Running time: 0.5–1 hour
Start altitude: 750 feet
Finish altitude: 750 feet
Elevation gain: 1,300 feet
Highest altitude: 1,960 feet
Difficulty: Strenuous
Water: None
Area management: Los Padres National Forest
    Pueblo Lands of Santa Barbara
Maps: Santa Barbara (USGS)
    Los Padres National Forest by the Forest Service

This challenging run goes along a stream and up fern-lined canyon switchbacks to scenic coastal views at the ridge. The stream has large boulders, tall sycamore trees, and thick ferns reminiscent of prehistoric times. Canyon views are excellent, and large oaks and bay laurel trees provide shade throughout the course.

GETTING THERE

From Highway 101 in Montecito, take Hot Springs Road north toward the mountains. At Mountain Drive, turn left. After 1.5 miles, cross Cold Springs Creek and park.

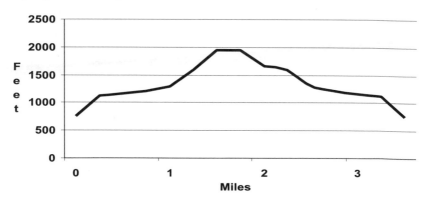

West Cold Springs Trail

THE RUN

Run north from the trailhead just east of the stream (4A). After 0.25 mile, the trail splits at a sign and a bench. Take the trail to the left that crosses the stream (4B) and continue up the west canyon wall. Ignore the trail that intersects from the right in 0.6 mile (4C) and continue left up to the paved Gibraltar Road, the turnaround point (4D). Cross the road to enjoy the coastal view. Return to the start the way you came.

SIGNIFICANT TRAIL LANDMARKS

4A. Trailhead east of the stream.

4B. Trail splits at a sign. Go left and cross the stream to west side of canyon.

4C. A trail intersects from the right. Continue left.

4D. Intersection with Gibraltar Road is the turnaround point. Return to the start the way you came.

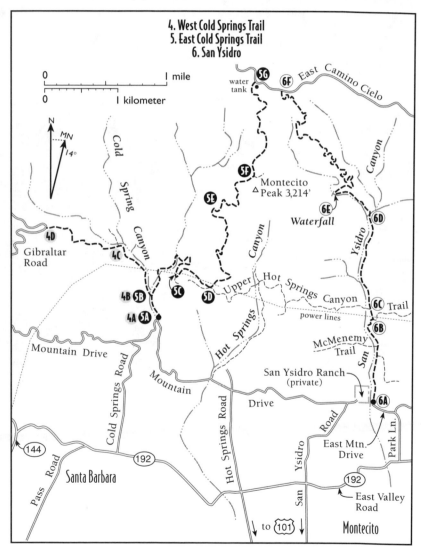

5

East Cold Springs Trail

Distance: 9 miles
Course geometry: Out and back
Running time: 1.5–3 hours
Start altitude: 750 feet
Finish altitude: 750 feet
Elevation gain: 2,800 feet
Highest altitude: 3,415 feet
Difficulty: Strenuous
Water: None
Area management: Pueblo Lands of Santa Barbara
    Los Padres National Forest
Maps: Santa Barbara (USGS)
    Los Padres National Forest by the Forest Service

This gorgeous course goes through a lush canyon with a bubbly stream, then up a fire road with vistas of Santa Barbara, the Channel Islands, and the Pacific Ocean. Ferns and vines line the numerous switchbacks. Stop and cool your feet in the rocky pools at the stream crossings. The fire road is exposed and can get hot. It also has many steep and rocky sections.

If your physical conditioning is average, you can turn around when you reach the fire road at the power line structures. If your conditioning is above average, you can continue up to the eucalyptus trees, and rest in the welcome

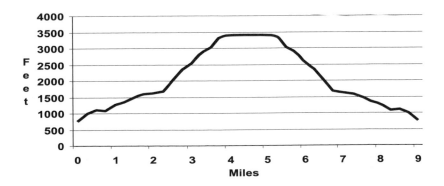

shade overlooking the Pacific Ocean. If you are in superior condition, you can continue to the top of the ridge with its views of the coastline and mountain ranges to the north. This run is inadvisable in hot weather as there is no water on the course.

GETTING THERE

From Highway 101 in Montecito, take Hot Springs Road north toward the mountains. At Mountain Drive, turn left. After 1.5 miles, cross Cold Springs Creek and park.

THE RUN

Stay to the east of the stream at the trailhead (5A). The West Cold Springs Trail branches to the left at about 0.25 mile (5B) and crosses the stream; make sure you stay to the right and continue straight ahead on the right bank. The course meanders in the canyon and is well shaded. When the trail takes a sharp left turn, an intersecting trail leads straight ahead. Continue to the left on the main trail (5C).

When you reach a fire road on the first ridge at mile 1.5 (5D), you can make a brief detour to the right up the ridge to enjoy the view of Santa Barbara. Return to the trail and continue left uphill in a northbound direction. About 100 yards farther on as you cross under the power lines, a single-track trail goes uphill to the left. Take this trail, avoiding the service road to the right. Some steep and rocky areas may require walking as you continue up this trail to the twin eucalyptus trees (5E) at elevation 2,480 feet. This is a nice spot to rest and savor your accomplishment.

Santa Barbara coastline view from East Cold Springs Trail

If you still have energy, continue up the trail to the top of the ridge. Along the way, watch for a trail (5F) to the right. Do not follow this. A paved access road (East Camino Cielo) and a water tank are at the top (5G). This is the turnaround point. Return to the start the way you came.

SIGNIFICANT TRAIL LANDMARKS

5A. Trailhead is east of the stream.

5B. West Cold Spring Trail branches to the left across the stream. Continue straight ahead on the right bank.

5C. Trail makes sharp turn to the left. Intersecting trail leads straight ahead. Stay on main trail.

5D. Intersection with a fire road at mile 1.5. Detour right to view Santa Barbara. Back at intersection, continue left uphill northbound. Go another 100 yards, cross under power lines, and take the smaller, steep trail on the left, avoiding the service road to the right.

5E. Twin eucalyptus trees.

5F. Secondary trail leads to the right. Stay to the left.

5G. Water tank and intersection with paved access road. Return to the start the way you came.

6

San Ysidro

Distance: 8.5 miles

Course geometry: Out and back

Running time: 1.25–2.5 hours

Start altitude: 440 feet

Finish altitude: 440 feet

Elevation gain: 3,100 feet

Highest altitude: 3,460 feet

Difficulty: Strenuous

Water: None

Area management: Pueblo Lands of Santa Barbara
   Los Padres National Forest

Maps: Santa Barbara (USGS)

This wonderful trail has a variety of vegetation and terrain, gorgeous views, and a spectacular waterfall. The lower part of the canyon is cool and lush,

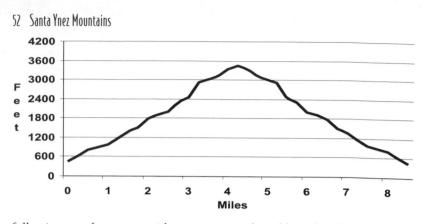

following a rocky stream with numerous pools and large boulders. Rest and refresh yourself at the waterfall, or if you have extra energy, you can continue up the trail to the ridge. This climb is challenging and all but the mightiest runners will have to walk certain sections. In the spring, the air is sweet with flowers blooming everywhere.

GETTING THERE

Driving south on Highway 101 from Santa Barbara, take the San Ysidro exit. Turn left at the stop sign and drive 1.1 miles to East Valley Road. Turn right and continue 0.9 mile to Park Lane. Turn left and continue for 0.4 mile to East Mountain Drive. Turn left on East Mountain Drive and proceed to the end of the street. Park away from any horse stables and do not park on the San Ysidro Ranch private property.

THE RUN

From the trailhead at the end of East Mountain Drive on the north side of the road (6A), proceed up the lush canyon along the stream for 2 miles. After 0.8 mile there is an intersection with a trail (6B) coming from the right; continue straight uphill.

In another 0.2 mile a fire road intersects from the left (6C), continue to the right on the smaller trail. The confluence of two streams (6D) at mile 1.75 force a water crossing. Cross over to the right (east) side of the stream and continue uphill keeping the stream to your left. Continue for another 0.5 mile until a switchback turns sharply to the right away from the stream. There is a small trail at the apex of this switchback that goes to a 30-foot waterfall landing in a nice size pool (6E). Refresh yourself here, and then continue up the trail another 2 miles to the ridge (6F). Enjoy tremendous views of the mountains, rock formations, and Santa Barbara from this delightful trail.

SIGNIFICANT TRAIL LAND-MARKS

6A. Trailhead at end of East Mountain Drive on north side of the road.

6B. Intersection with a trail from the right. Continue straight ahead.

6C. Intersection with fire road. Take the smaller road to the right.

6D. Two streams converge. Cross to right side of stream and continue uphill following the stream.

6E. Trail turns right sharply away from the stream. Continue straight 30 feet to waterfall.

6F. Turn around at the ridge and return the way you came.

Waterfall at San Ysidro

Romero Canyon

Distance: 13.5 miles
Course geometry: Out and back
Running time: 1.75–3.25 hours
Start altitude: 925 feet
Finish altitude: 925 feet
Elevation gain: 2,500 feet
Highest altitude: 3,100 feet
Difficulty: Strenuous
Water: None
Area management: Los Padres National Forest
Maps: Carpinteria (USGS)

The steady climb up the Romero Canyon Road offers dramatic views of the Pacific Ocean and coastline, as well as a rewarding panorama of the magnificent

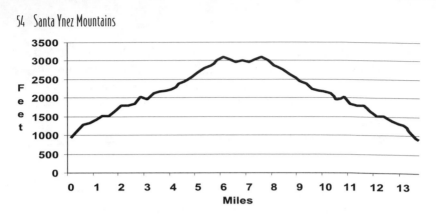

northern mountain ranges when you get to the top of the course. Early portions of the climb are under canopies of shrubbery and feature seasonal wildflowers. The course is rocky in some areas. East Camino Cielo, a paved road, is at the top in case you want to shorten the run and make it a point-to-point course. On a clear day, bring a camera to this Santa Barbara favorite.

GETTING THERE

Driving south on Highway 101 from Santa Barbara, take the Sheffield Drive exit. Follow Sheffield Drive north 1.5 miles to East Valley Road. Turn left on East Valley Road and in 50 yards turn right on Romero Canyon Road. Proceed 1.5 miles north on Romero Canyon Road. Stay to the right at the fork in this road, then turn right on Bella Vista Drive. Park 0.3 mile down the road, near the red steel gate on the left.

THE RUN

Head north around the red gate at the trailhead (7A). The first half-mile is steeper than the rest of the run, so take it easy. At mile 0.25, you will cross a bridge over Romero Canyon Creek (7B) and then a stream (7C). One hundred feet past the stream, the small Romero Canyon Trail intersects on the left. Continue on the main fire road to the right. As you climb this fire road, it boggles the imagination to realize that wagons and old cars used to struggle up this same road to make it to the other side of the mountain.

Another fire road intersects on the right at mile 2 near the powerlines (7D). Continue to the left on the main fire road, passing under the powerlines. The fire road narrows shortly to become a single-track trail, followed by small stream crossings at mile 2.2 (7E) and at mile 3.4 (7F).

At mile 4, there is an intersection with the smaller Romero Canyon Trail (7G); continue straight uphill on the main trail. Now the trail becomes more exposed to the sun. The widening views of the fabulous coastline are excellent.

There is a wide clearing with a water tank (7H) off to the right at mile 6.25. Continue due north. The trail ends near a 5,000-gallon water tank at East Camino Cielo (7I), just as the mountain ranges to the north come into view. After appreciating the view from here, return to the start the way you came.

SIGNIFICANT TRAIL LANDMARKS

7A. Trailhead at red gate.

7B. Bridge crossing.

7C. Stream crossing followed by intersection with small Romero Canyon Trail to the left. Continue to the right on the fire road.

7D. Intersection with fire road at mile 2. Continue to the left on main fire road, passing under powerlines. Road soon becomes single-track trail.

7E. Stream crossing at mile 2.2.

7F. Stream crossing at mile 3.4.

7G. Intersection with Romero Canyon Trail. Continue straight uphill on main trail.

7H. Wide clearing and water tank. Continue due north.

7I. Second water tank and trail's end at East Camino Cielo. Return to the start the way you came.

Romero Canyon

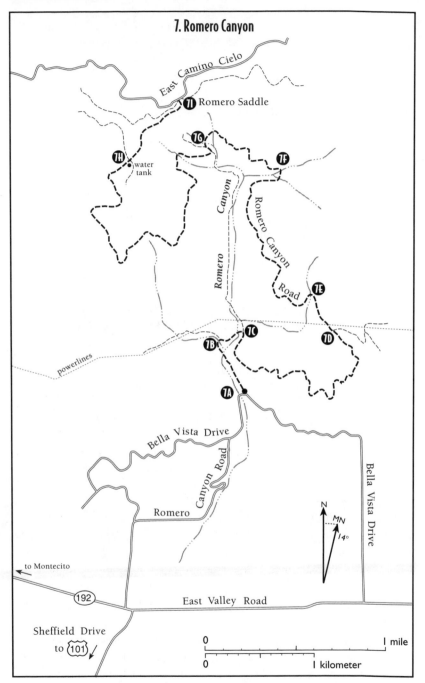

7. Romero Canyon

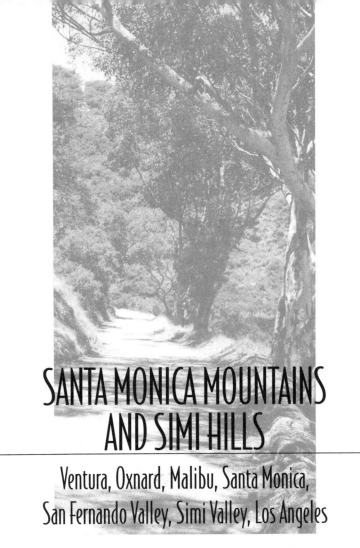

SANTA MONICA MOUNTAINS AND SIMI HILLS

Ventura, Oxnard, Malibu, Santa Monica, San Fernando Valley, Simi Valley, Los Angeles

The Santa Monica Mountains are located in the heart of the Los Angeles Basin. These beautiful mountains begin at Point Mugu near Oxnard and end in Griffith Park near Hollywood. They are close to major population centers including Oxnard, the Conejo Valley, the San Fernando Valley, Los Angeles, Santa Monica, Pacific Palisades, and Malibu. These accessible mountains are an ideal escape to peaceful and natural settings for trail running. Encroaching development has taken its toll in several places, but many large areas are preserved for nature and recreation.

The Santa Monica Range is about 10 miles wide and nearly 50 miles long. The highest point is Sandstone Peak at 3,111 feet. A variety of terrain is waiting to be discovered, including high ridges with rocky trails and great views of Los Angeles, Santa Monica, Pacific Palisades, the San Fernando Valley, the ocean, and lush canyons with numerous streams, smooth meadows, and rolling hills.

Riparian woodlands, coastal sage, grasslands, and chaparral blend together to form a unique and picturesque environment.

Ray Miller Trail

Distance: 10.7 miles
Course geometry: Loop
Running time: 1.5–3 hours
Start altitude: 50 feet
Finish altitude: 50 feet
Elevation gain: 1,500 feet
Highest altitude: 1,050 feet
Difficulty: Moderate
Water: At the start and finish
Area management: Point Mugu State Park
Maps: Point Mugu (USGS)
     Trail Map of the Santa Monica Mountains, West

If you can only run two trails in Southern California, one should be the Ray Miller Trail and the other should be the Ray Miller Trail in the opposite direction. This extraordinary course has well-maintained trails, spectacular ocean and mountain views, and a variety of challenging terrain. The paved parking lot is right at the trailhead with water, picnic tables, and restrooms— welcome sights following the run.

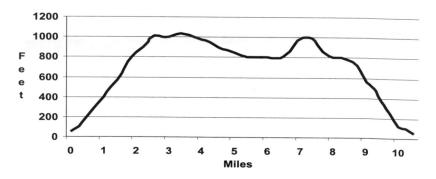

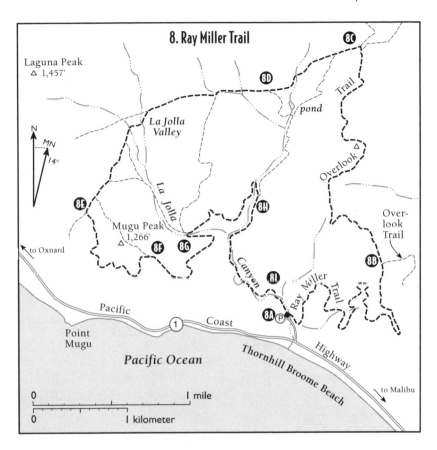

8. Ray Miller Trail

Laguna Peak
△ 1,457'

N

MN

14°

La Jolla
Valley

pond

Trail

Overlook

△

Over-
look
Trail

8E

Mugu Peak
△ 1,266'

8F

8G

8H

to Oxnard

8B

Canyon

8I

Ray Miller

Trail

Pacific

Coast

8A P

Point
Mugu

Highway

Pacific Ocean

Thornhill Broome Beach

1

to Malibu

0   1 mile
0   1 kilometer

GETTING THERE

From Santa Monica, drive north on Pacific Coast Highway toward Malibu. Twenty-one miles north of Malibu Canyon Road you will come to Thornhill Broome Beach. Look for the big sand dune on the hill to your right. One mile north of the sand dune, turn right off the highway into La Jolla Canyon. Drive to the main parking lot up the road to the left. The parking fee is $2.

THE RUN

The Ray Miller trailhead (8A) is across the road to your right, near the northeast end of the parking lot. For the first 2.7 miles the trail climbs 1,000 feet through chaparral, providing dazzling views of the coastline the higher you ascend. You can hear the waves breaking on the rocks and sand below.

The well-defined trail winds its way around ridges in a series of long switchbacks, ending at a fire road (8B). Turn left onto the fire road and enjoy the views in both directions. To the right is Sycamore Canyon and in the distance you can see Sandstone Peak, the tallest mountain in the Santa Monica Range. Farther along and to the left, a wide valley is filled with grass-covered meadows and trees growing along a small streambed. The fire road leads to a trail that takes you through this valley.

Two miles from where you turned onto the fire road you will arrive at a four-way intersection (8C). Turn left and run downhill into the valley. Soon the fire road becomes a narrower trail that passes walk-in campsites in the middle of this lovely, 600-acre grassland. Chemical toilets are located here at campsites 4 through 11 (8D).

Although always passable, the section of trail after the campsites can be somewhat overgrown with grass, especially in the spring and summer months. Keep an eye out for rattlesnakes and hidden holes and rocks as the grass makes visibility difficult. If you are running in the spring or early summer, stop for a while to enjoy the many flowers and birds. Stay on the main trail and avoid any trails that veer to the left or the right or that significantly change the direction you have been heading. Keep the hillside with the large white antennas to your right and head for the saddle between the hills straight ahead.

The trail out of the valley ascends the right side of Mugu Peak. At mile 6.9 when you can see the ocean 1000 feet below (8E), take the trail to the left. The trail to the right drops steeply to Pacific Coast Highway. For the next 1.8 miles the trail winds around Mugu Peak and again offers spectacular ocean and mountain views and great photo opportunities. You will see several varieties of cactus along this rocky section. Trails intersect from the left, but stay to the right on the main trail (8F).

After 1 mile, you will be able to see La Jolla Canyon below and directly ahead. The trail makes a turn to the left as you begin to descend into the upper section of La Jolla Canyon. Be careful as you descend the steep and often rocky trail, which in spring can be quite overgrown with vegetation. Eventually, the trail leads to the first of five stream crossings (8G). These areas have poison oak growing near the trail. Immediately after crossing the first stream, turn right across a flat field. You will see the trail continuing on the hill directly in front of you. Climb the short hill and quickly descend into the canyon and then cross the stream a second time. A short distance from the stream, another trail joins on the left (8H). Stay right and continue down into upper La Jolla Canyon.

For the next mile, the trail follows the left side of the stream over exposed, rocky switchbacks. At one point, the trail almost disappears where large boulders block it. Scramble to the right to find the trail again. A few hundred feet

La Jolla Valley

farther, you cross the stream again below a waterfall that fills a shady green pool (8I). After passing the waterfall and pool, the trail continues downhill, crossing the stream twice more before returning to the La Jolla Canyon parking area where you began.

Option: In La Jolla Valley at miles 4.9, 5.1, 5.3, 5.7, and 6.4, there are trails that go off to the left (see map) and which eventually return to the main trail without taking you around Mugu Peak. These trails reduce the overall mileage. They are all wonderful trails, but you will not have the superb ocean views as you round Point Mugu.

SIGNIFICANT TRAIL LANDMARKS

- 8A. Trailhead directly across from parking lot to the northeast.
- 8B. Climb 2.7 miles to intersection with a fire road. Turn left onto road.
- 8C. Four-way intersection. Turn left headed downhill.
- 8D. Chemical toilets.
- 8E. The ocean comes into view at mile 6.9. Take the trail to the left.
- 8F. Trail winds around Mugu Peak. Stay to the right at intersections with trails from the left.
- 8G. Steep, rocky trail leads to stream crossing at mile 8.7. Cross stream and turn right across field.
- 8H. Intersection with trail from the left. Stay right and descend into canyon.
- 8I. Stream crossing and waterfall. Trail continues downhill to the parking lot.

9

Sycamore Canyon to La Jolla Valley Loop

Distance: 11.75 miles
Course geometry: Out-and-back loop
Running time: 1.75–3.25 hours
Start altitude: 70 feet
Finish altitude: 70 feet
Elevation gain: 1,675 feet
Highest altitude: 1,100 feet
Difficulty: Moderate
Water: At the start and finish
Area management: Point Mugu State Park
Maps: Point Mugu (USGS)
　　　Trail Map of the Santa Monica Mountains, West

This course features challenging climbs over a variety of terrain with excellent views of the ocean, peaks, and valleys. The course shares some of the same fire roads and trails as the Ray Miller Trail. A combination of wide fire roads and narrow trails adds variety to this exciting and adventurous run. There are restrooms, sinks, and showers near the parking lot and in the nearby campground. A public beach is just across Pacific Coast Highway.

GETTING THERE
From Santa Monica, drive 32 miles north on Pacific Coast Highway to Sycamore Canyon. Look for several large directional signs and turn right onto the road leading into the canyon. Follow it past the park entrance, then turn

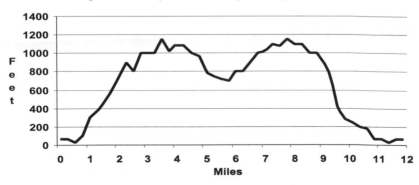

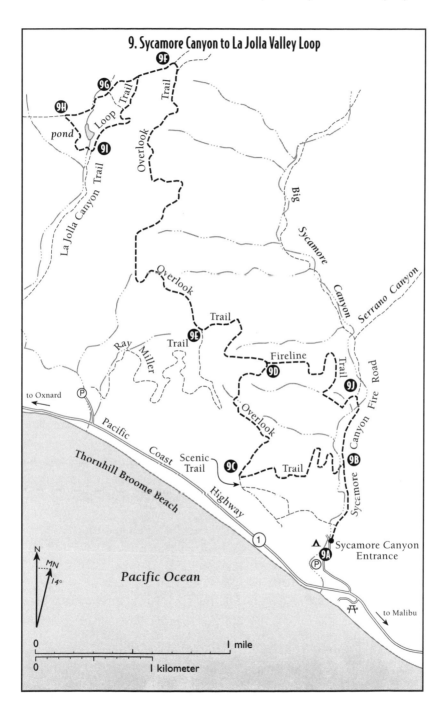

9. Sycamore Canyon to La Jolla Valley Loop

9F

9G

9H

Loop Trail

Trail

pond

9I

Overlook

La Jolla Canyon Trail

Big

Sycamore

Canyon

Serrano Canyon

Overlook

Trail

9E

Trail

Ray Miller

Trail

Fireline

9D

Trail

9J

Sycamore Canyon Fire Road

Overlook

to Oxnard

P

Pacific

Coast

Scenic
Trail

9C

Trail

9B

Thornhill Broome Beach

Highway

1

Sycamore Canyon
Entrance

9A

P

to Malibu

N

MN

14°

Pacific Ocean

0   I mile

0   I kilometer

left into the parking area. Parking is $6. Some parking is available on Pacific Coast Highway, but take care to observe posted parking restrictions.

THE RUN

From the parking lot, run north through the campground on the paved road that leads to a fire road behind a wooden gate (9A). Forty yards after the gate a trail leads away to the left. This is called the Scenic Trail. Continue straight on the main road. In 0.75 miles turn left onto the Overlook Trail (9B). The trail begins to climb out of the canyon in a series of moderately steep switchbacks. In just over 1 mile, the trail intersects with the Scenic Trail leading away to the left (9C). Continue to the right as the Overlook Trail winds up and around the gentle contours of the hillside. Enjoy the wonderful views down into Sycamore Canyon and beyond to the peaks of Boney Mountain.

One mile farther at a sharp left bend is the Fireline Trail that leads away to the right (9D). Later you will follow this trail to return to the canyon. For now, continue on the main trail. At mile 3, the Ray Miller Trail intersects from the left (9E) as it follows the ridge with Sycamore Canyon on the right and La Jolla Canyon on the left. Continue straight to follow the Overlook Trail. In 2 miles, a narrow trail branches off to the right leading back down into Sycamore Canyon. Continue straight to a wide, four-way intersection 50 yards farther on (9F). The fire road to the right leads down into Wood Canyon. The middle trail leads to the Guadalasca Trail. Take the trail downhill to the left leading into the La Jolla Valley Natural Reserve.

Follow the main trail west, avoiding any trails leading away to the left or the right. In 0.6 mile, after passing campgrounds on the right (9G), a small trail leads away on the left. Turn left here and follow the signs pointing the way to Highway 1. Turn left at the fork 100 yards up the trail (9H). This short, 0.2-mile trail follows a small creekbed, which turns into a lovely pond. Thoughtful reflection is possible in this quiet setting.

Shortly after crossing the stream, the trail dead-ends at the La Jolla Canyon Trail (9I). Turn left and follow it for 0.6 mile to where it joins the Loop Trail, which leads back to the Overlook Trail.

Back on the Overlook Trail, retrace the course for 2.5 miles until you reach the Fireline Trail (9D) on the left. Take this trail. The first 100 yards is very steep, but then curves to the left to begin a series of long, gentle switchbacks that follow the contours of the hills into the canyon directly below. The Fireline Trail dead-ends after 0.75 mile at the bottom of Sycamore Canyon (9J). Turn right and return to the start in 0.75 mile.

Canopy of trees

SIGNIFICANT TRAIL LANDMARKS

9A. Trailhead behind wood fence at the north end of paved road through campground.

9B. Scenic Trail veers left. Continue on road to the Overlook Trail at 0.75 mile. Go left onto Overlook Trail.

9C. Junction with Scenic Trail on the left. Continue uphill to the right.

9D. Intersection with Fireline Trail at mile 2.3. Continue left on the main fire road, but note entrance to Fireline Trail for return trip.

9E. Junction with Ray Miller Trail on the left at mile 3. Continue straight on Overlook Trail.

9F. Four-way intersection. Turn left downhill.

9G. Pass campsites at miles 5.6 and 5.7.

9H. Turn left at sign pointing to Highway 1. In 100 yards, turn left again at fork.

9I. Trail dead-ends at La Jolla Canyon Trail. Turn left to join Loop Trail, which leads back to the Overlook Trail. Retrace route to a left turn onto Fireline Trail (D).

9J. Fireline Trail dead-ends at the bottom of Sycamore Canyon. Turn right and return to the start.

10
Sycamore Canyon Loop

Distance: 12 miles

Course geometry: Out-and-back loop

Running time: 1.5–3 hours

Start altitude: 70 feet

Finish altitude: 70 feet

Elevation gain: 750 feet

Highest altitude: 775 feet

Difficulty: Moderate

Water: At the start and finish and point I

Area management: Point Mugu State Park

Maps: Point Mugu, Trifuno, and Newbury Park (USGS)
Trail Map of the Santa Monica Mountains, West

The trail begins after passing campsites that flank the beginning of Sycamore Canyon. While climbing the fire roads along the gently rising canyon, the

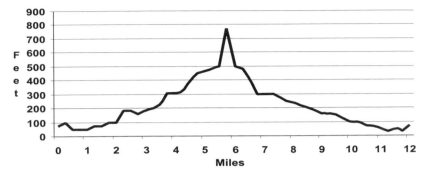

sycamore trees gradually give way to mature oak trees and chaparral. This canyon can be quite cool in the fall and winter, so dress accordingly. There is a pay phone and a toilet at point F and water is available 0.5 mile off the course at point I. There are restrooms, sinks, and an outdoor shower near the parking lot at the finish. A sandy public beach is just across the highway.

GETTING THERE

From Santa Monica, drive 32 miles north on Pacific Coast Highway to Sycamore Canyon. Look for several large directional signs and turn right onto the road leading into the canyon. Follow it past the park entrance, then turn left into the parking area. Parking is $6. Some parking is available on Pacific Coast Highway, but take care to observe posted parking restrictions.

THE RUN

From the parking lot, run north through the campground on the paved road that leads to a fire road behind a wooden gate (10A). You will remain on the main dirt road for 3 miles. There are several shallow water crossings in this initial 3-mile stretch. Watch for deer and other small animals that come to drink in the streams.

At mile 1, the Serrano Canyon Trail joins on the right (10B); continue to the left. At mile 3, there is a wide-open area with trail signs. Big Sycamore Canyon Fire Road continues to the right; turn left onto Wood Canyon Fire Road (10C).

At mile 3.5, remain on the dirt road leading to the right at the intersection with the Overlook Fire Road (10D). At mile 3.8, stay to the right at the intersection with the Guadalasca Trail emerging on the left (10E). Signposts mark the trail and these intersecting dirt roads are well established.

Rustic wooden structures stand out at mile 5.1 (10F). This is a park

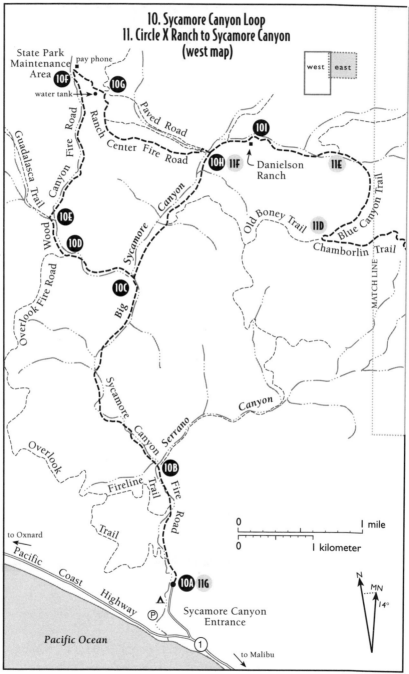

10. Sycamore Canyon Loop
11. Circle X Ranch to Sycamore Canyon
(west map)

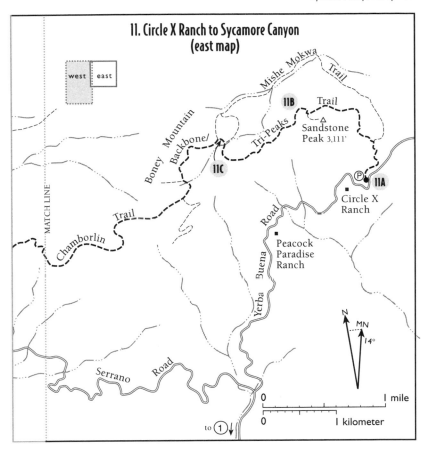

11. Circle X Ranch to Sycamore Canyon (east map)

maintenance area with a pay phone and a portable toilet. The dirt road ends and becomes a paved service road here. Turn right on this paved road and continue up the hill for 0.3 mile. Cattle grazing on the surrounding hillsides calmly watch as you run by. There is an old hilltop water tank on the right at mile 5.6 (10G). Immediately after the water tank, take the Ranch Center Fire Road going downhill on the right back to Big Sycamore Canyon. Turn right on Big Sycamore Canyon Fire Road (10H).

Option: If you want water with shaded tables and benches, instead of going right on Big Sycamore Canyon Fire Road, continue straight ahead 100 yards and turn left to Danielson Ranch (10I). This 1-mile round trip offers a welcome stop on a hot day.

Return south down the main dirt road in the canyon for another 4.5 miles from point I back to the parking lot.

Sycamore Canyon (Photo by Phil Bailey)

SIGNIFICANT TRAIL LANDMARKS

10A. Trailhead behind wood gate at the north end of campground.

10B. Intersection of Serrano Canyon Trail from the right. Continue left.

10C. At mile 3, turn left onto Wood Canyon Fire Road.

10D. Intersection with the Overlook Fire Road. Stay to the right on the dirt road.

10E. Junction with Guadalasca Trail on the left. Stay right.

10F. Park maintenance area at mile 5.1. End of dirt road; turn right onto paved service road.

10G. At mile 5.6, turn right onto Ranch Center Fire Road immediately after water tank.

10H. Intersection with Sycamore Canyon Fire Road at mile 6.6. Turn right to return to the start. Alternatively, continue straight ahead approximately 100 yards and turn left, then veer to the right for water at Danielson Ranch.

10I. Go 0.5 mile to Danielson Ranch for water and a shady place to rest.

11

Circle X Ranch to Sycamore Canyon

Distance: 12 miles
Course geometry: Point to point
Running time: 1.75–3.25 hours
Start altitude: 2,030 feet
Finish altitude: 70 feet
Elevation gain: 1,200 feet
Highest altitude: 3,111 feet
Difficulty: Strenuous
Water: At Danielson Ranch and the finish
Area management: Point Mugu State Park
Maps: Point Mugu (USGS)
> Trail Map of the Santa Monica Mountains, West
> Trail Illustrated Santa Monica Mountains National Recreation Area

Panoramic views with interesting rock formations highlight the early part of this tough course. A short detour from the main trail 1.3 miles from the start leads to Sandstone Peak, the highest peak in the Santa Monica Mountains, with great views in all directions. Heavy foliage in the middle section can sometimes make running difficult; long sleeves and protective leggings are recommended. The final 4.4 miles through Sycamore Canyon requires several stream crossings under large, beautiful trees. There are picnic tables, restrooms, and an outdoor shower near the campsite area. The beach is directly across Pacific Coast Highway if you feel an urge for a post run swim

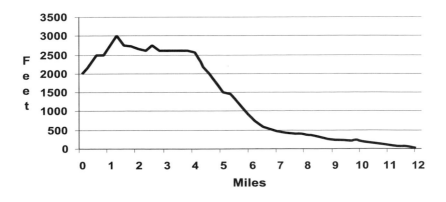

GETTING THERE

From Santa Monica, drive 32 miles north on Pacific Coast Highway to Sycamore Canyon. Look for several large directional signs and turn right onto the road leading into the canyon. Follow it past the park entrance, then turn left into the parking area. Parking is $6. Some parking is available on Pacific Coast Highway, but take care to observe posted parking restrictions.

With a second vehicle, from Sycamore Canyon drive south 3.3 miles on Pacific Coast Highway to Yerba Buena Road and turn left. Drive 6 miles uphill past Peacock Paradise Ranch (4.1 miles) and Circle X Ranch (5.7 miles) to the small dirt Backbone Trail parking area on the left approximately 0.25 mile beyond Circle X Ranch.

THE RUN

The trail begins with a steep climb from the north end of the parking area (11A). You will shortly pass a sign that marks the Mishe Mokwa Trail leading to the right. Continue uphill on the main trail to the left. After crossing to the north side of the ridge 1.3 miles from the start and just before the main trail takes a sharp right U-turn, a narrow trail on the left leads up to the sum-

Climbing toward Sandstone Peak

mit of Sandstone Peak (11B). At 3,111 feet, Sandstone Peak stands as the highest point in the Santa Monica Range. It is worth a detour up this steep, 0.2-mile trail for the incredible 360-degree views from the summit. After capturing the summit, pause a few minutes to record your impressions in the logbook kept at the monument.

Return to the main trail and continue west along the ridge, winding between sandstone outcroppings. The trail forks 2.3 miles from the start with a second intersection with the Mishe Mokwa Trail (11C) on the right. Continue left on the Backbone/Tri-Peaks Trail. Thirty yards farther on, the trail forks again. Follow the Chamborlin Trail to the left. It is 5 miles to Sycamore Canyon from here. A short distance down the trail, it forks again. Take the left fork on the Chamborlin Trail leading to Sycamore Canyon.

When approaching the section of trail that leads down into Sycamore Canyon, the views of the Oxnard plain become increasingly dramatic. Running on the trail here can be difficult because heavy brush can reach more than 7-feet tall. If the vegetation obscures the trail, take care to avoid unseen obstacles at your feet. Think of it as an adventure and have fun.

Eventually the brush clears and the trail is clearly visible following a ridge to the west. Just before getting to the ridge you pass a large rock on the right and negotiate two consecutive 180-degree curves, first to the left and then to the right. Descend to a trail junction. The Old Boney Trail goes to the left and Blue Canyon Trail goes to the right (11D). Take the Blue Canyon Trail heading north downhill before turning west (11E). It eventually leads to Danielson Ranch (11F), which has a small picnic area with a large, stone fireplace and a water fountain. On hot days, cool off in the shade of the oak trees while watching for deer feeding and drinking from the nearby stream.

From Danielson Ranch, a flat 5-mile run through Sycamore Canyon leads to the finish. Expect several stream crossings. The trail ends in the Sycamore Canyon camping area (11G).

SIGNIFICANT TRAIL LANDMARKS

11A. Trailhead at the north end of the parking area.

11B. At 1.3 miles, look to the left for the 0.2-mile side trail to Sandstone Peak.

11C. Second intersection with the Mishe Mokwa Trail. Stay left on the Backbone/Tri-Peaks Trail.

11D. Junction of three trails. Take the Blue Canyon Trail to the right.

11E. At 6.8 miles, the Blue Canyon Trail turns west toward Sycamore Canyon.

11F. Danielson Ranch has water near a stone fireplace.

11G. Sycamore Canyon camping area. Continue down the road to your car.

12

Latigo Canyon to Tapia Park

Distance: 11.5 miles
Course geometry: Point to point
Running time: 1.5–3 hours
Start altitude: 2,075 feet
Finish altitude: 480 feet
Elevation gain: 1,400 feet
Highest altitude: 2,320 feet
Difficulty: Moderate
Water: None
Area management: National Park Service
    California Department of Parks and Recreation
Maps: Point Dume and Malibu Beach (USGS)
    Trail Map of the Santa Monica Mountains, Central

This beautiful course crosses mountain crests with views of the coastline, the Channel Islands to the southeast, and the valleys and mountain ranges to the north. There are stunning rock formations along the ridge, including the famous Bulldog Rock. The trail begins in cool, shaded canyons, and then continues mostly on fire roads with dense shrubbery and oak trees. Short climbs and descents make this run challenging even though it is largely downhill. Driving 14 miles from the finish to the start is necessary to set up this run, but the rewards are worth the extra effort.

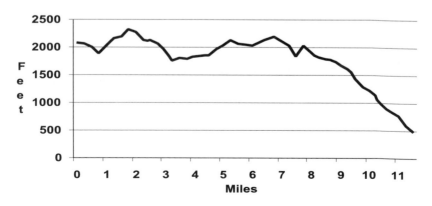

Overlooking Malibu Canyon

GETTING THERE

Take Malibu Canyon Road north from Pacific Coast Highway or take Las Virgenes Road south from the Ventura Freeway (Interstate 101) and turn west into Tapia Park, which is 3 miles south of Mulholland Highway. Parking is $5. Leave a car at Tapia Park, then take a second car and drive north on Malibu Canyon Road to Mulholland Highway and turn left (west). Continue approximately 8.75 miles to Kanan Dume Road, turn left and drive 0.75 mile south to Latigo Canyon Road and turn left again. Drive 2.5 miles and park in the small, dirt parking area on the left (12A).

THE RUN

The trailhead at the north end of the parking area is marked with a signpost indicating it is part of the Backbone Trail (12A). The trail climbs up a short hill followed by a descent into the upper section of Newton Canyon. After a rain, prepare to get wet from the water-soaked grass lining both sides of the trail. At the bottom of the canyon, a sharp turn marks the beginning of the next climb leading to a fire road 1.4 miles from the start (12B). Several sections leading to the fire road are steep, so take care to watch for loose rocks. There is little shade here, and it can get quite hot in the summer. Catalina Island and the blue Pacific Ocean are visible to the south.

Turn right at the fire road and make an immediate left on a trail leading downhill into the upper section of Solstice Canyon. Descend on a series of switchbacks and follow the trail east as it crosses the stream under a lush

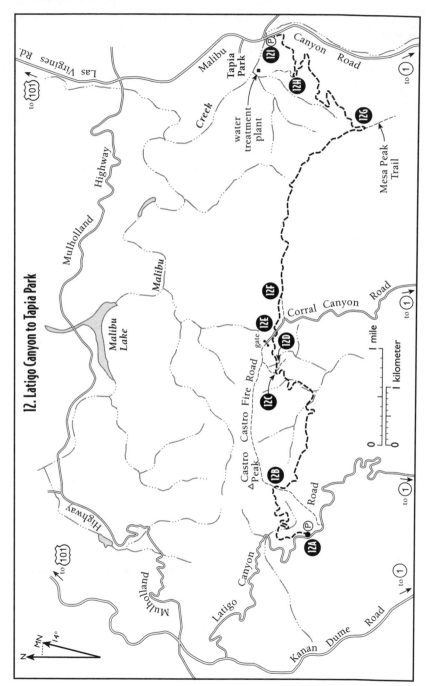

12. Latigo Canyon to Tapia Park

canopy of trees. The trail eventually turns north as it climbs gently out of the canyon. At an intersection with a little-used fire road (12C), turn right onto the road. Follow the fire road and pick up the trail on the left side of the fire road around a bend. The trail again heads east through the chaparral. Continue downhill for 300 yards and watch carefully for a narrower trail to the left marked with a Backbone Trail sign. Turn left on this trail (12D). At mile 4.2, the trail ends at a large, dirt parking area at the top of Corral Canyon Road (12E).

The trail picks up again to the east across the parking area. Continue uphill toward the three large rock formations along the ridge to the east. At 0.5 mile from the Corral Canyon parking area, look for the small stand of eucalyptus trees and pass below them on the left. Shortly after passing the eucalyptus trees, climb up the large sandstone rock directly ahead. At the top of this short climb, take the trail to the left as it turns north and then east again. A steep descent leads back to the fire road (12F). Turn left on the fire road and continue east.

This fire road leads along the ridge and back down into Malibu Canyon on a series of long, steep switchbacks. Just before descending, the switchbacks on the north side of the ridge pass the Mesa Peak Trail leading to the right (12G). A steep trail takes you over a landslide that was not cleared near this intersection.

Near the bottom of the canyon, look carefully for a small trail leading to the right as you round a sharp right turn on the fire road. Take this trail uphill (12H) as it winds back to the parking area on Malibu Canyon Road (12I).

SIGNIFICANT TRAIL LANDMARKS
12A. Trailhead at north end of parking area.
12B. Intersection with fire road. Turn right on road and then immediately left onto trail.
12C. Turn right onto fire road and pick up the trail on the left around the bend.
12D. Turn left onto the Backbone Trail.
12E. Cross the Corral Canyon parking area to the east and head toward the large rock formations.
12F. Steep descent to main fire road. Turn left onto road heading east.
12G. Mesa Peak Trail on the right before descent into Malibu Canyon.
12H. Near the bottom of the canyon, turn right onto narrow trail going uphill.
12I. Parking area on Malibu Canyon Road.

13
Tapia Park to Century Reservoir

Distance: 6 miles
Course geometry: Out and back
Running time: 1–1.5 hours
Start altitude: 480 feet
Finish altitude: 480 feet
Elevation gain: 900 feet
Highest altitude: 770 feet
Difficulty: Easy
Water: At locations 13E, 13G, and 13I
Area management: National Park Service
    California Department of Parks and Recreation
Maps: Malibu Beach (USGS)
    Trail Map of the Santa Monica Mountains, Central
    Trails Illustrated Santa Monica Mountains National Recreation Area

The course begins in oak-filled Tapia Park located in the middle of Malibu Canyon, and includes moderate climbs and level sections along Malibu Creek. Along with sweeping hilltop views of the surrounding valleys and mountains, you may see deer grazing in the meadows and ducks in the slow-moving creek. An abundance of shade and water fountains makes this a great hot-weather run. Water is available at map locations 13E, 13G, and 13I. For additional mileage, combine this run with other local trails.

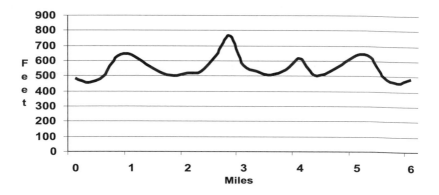

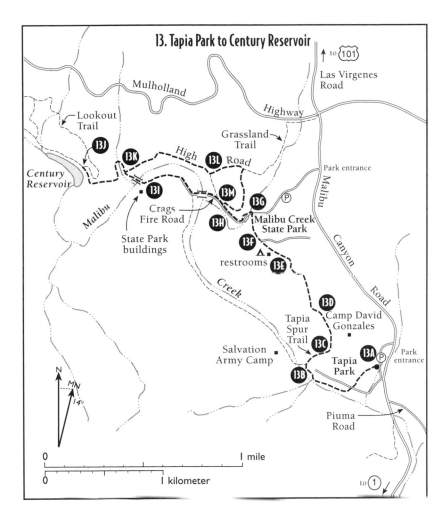

GETTING THERE

Take Malibu Canyon Road north from the Pacific Coast Highway or take Las Virgenes Road south from the Ventura Freeway (Interstate 101) and turn into Tapia Park, which is 3 miles south of Mulholland Highway. Parking is $5.

THE RUN

The trailhead is at the west end of the south parking lot (13A). Pass through the gate and take the dirt road heading west that parallels the paved road on the right. At mile 0.3, the dirt road joins a paved road near the entrance

Malibu Creek

to the Salvation Army Camp (13B). Cross the paved road and take the narrow trail that is 40 yards from the Salvation Army camp entrance on the
left. This begins the 0.9-mile long Tapia Spur Trail leading to Malibu Creek
State Park.

At mile 0.5, the trail makes a sharp left turn up the hill (13C). There is a
signpost identifying this as the Backbone Trail. Camp David Gonzales is visible below on the right (13D). The trail curves to the left at the top of the
hill and then descends into Malibu Creek State Park. As the trail flattens out
at the bottom of the hill, stay to the right of the campground restrooms and
continue on the trail on the left side of the dirt road (13E).

At mile 1.3, turn left at the intersection with the paved road (13F) and run on the trail on the left side of this road. At mile 1.5, turn left on Crags Fire Road, which crosses Malibu Creek (13G). Continue on the short stretch of paved road and at mile 1.7 take the dirt road to the left at the wide intersection. Cross another bridge and at the intersection with another wide dirt road turn right (13H).

At mile 2.2, pass the buildings on the left (13I). Turn right, cross a large bridge, and continue straight uphill on the High Road, which intersects from the right. After reaching the top of the hill, the Century Reservoir is to the left (13J). This blue body of water surrounded by steep cliffs is a sparkling gem. It is also the turnaround point for this run.

On the return, instead of crossing the bridge approaching the park buildings, turn left onto the High Road at mile 3.2 (13K). At mile 3.7, the High Road veers to the right and a trail intersects from the left (13L). Take the trail up the hill and turn right at the top to take the Grasslands Trail back to Malibu Creek State Park. Turn left at Crags Fire Road and return to the start on the same course.

SIGNIFICANT TRAIL LANDMARKS

13A. Trailhead at west end of south parking lot.

13B. Dirt road joins paved road near the Salvation Army Camp. Cross road to narrow Tapia Spur Trail 40 yards from camp entrance.

13C. Trail makes a sharp left turn and begins to climb. Sign identifies Backbone Trail.

13D. Pass Camp David Gonzales.

13E. Enter Malibu Creek State Park. Stay to right of restrooms.

13F. Intersection with paved road at mile 1.3. Turn left onto trail paralleling left side of road.

13G. Turn left onto Crags Fire Road at mile 1.5.

13H. At mile 1.7, take dirt road to the left at the wide intersection. Cross bridge and turn right onto another dirt road.

13I. Pass park buildings on left at mile 2.2. Cross bridge and continue straight uphill on High Road.

13J. Century Reservoir on the left. This is the turnaround point.

13K. At mile 3.2 on the return, turn left onto High Road before the bridge.

13L. At mile 3.7, take the narrow trail to the left uphill.

13M. At top of hill, turn right onto Grasslands Trail and continue to Crags Fire Road. Turn left and return to the start the same way you came.

14

Malibu Creek State Park to Paramount Ranch

Distance: 8 miles
Course geometry: Out and back
Running time: 1.25–2 hours
Start altitude: 600 feet
Finish altitude: 600 feet
Elevation gain: 1,200 feet
Highest altitude: 930 feet
Difficulty: Easy
Water: At map locations 14D, 14G, and 14I
Area management: National Park Service
    California Department of Parks and Recreation
Maps: Point Dume and Malibu Beach (USGS)
    Trail Map of the Santa Monica Mountains, Central
    Trails Illustrated Santa Monica Mountains National Recreation Area

Some of the higher ridges and peaks of the Santa Monica Mountains surround Malibu Creek State Park in Malibu Canyon. This run follows Malibu Creek and surrounding grass-filled meadows. The Paramount Ranch television and movie set has a re-creation of a western town and is the turnaround point for this course. Exploring the western movie town will capture your imagination.

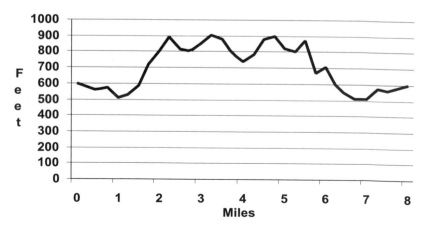

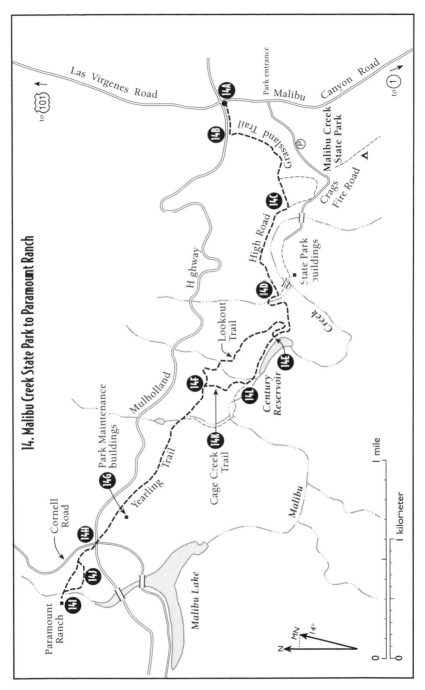

14. Malibu Creek State Park to Paramount Ranch

GETTING THERE

From the Ventura Freeway (Interstate 101), take the Las Virgenes Road exit and drive south to the intersection with Mulholland Highway. Park near the intersection where space is available and unrestricted. Additional parking is available in the Malibu Creek parking lot just south of Mulholland Highway for $5, and north of Mulholland Highway on the west side of Las Virgenes Road.

From Pacific Coast Highway, take Malibu Canyon Road north to the intersection with Mulholland Highway, and park (14A).

THE RUN

The trailhead is located on the south side of Mulholland Highway 260 yards west of Las Virgenes Road (14B). Look for the opening in the chain-link fence. The first 0.5 mile leads through rolling, grass-covered hills ending at the top of a hill overlooking Triunfo Canyon and Malibu Creek.

At the bottom of the hill, turn right onto the High Road (14C). You may see ducks and other wildlife as you run under broad oak trees along Malibu Creek. At the end of this creek near a bridge, Crags Fire Road intersects from the left (14D). Continue to the right on Crags Fire Road as it climbs up a steep hill. Just over the top of this hill overlooking Century Reservoir at mile 1.8, the Lookout Trail (14E) intersects from the right. Take this narrow trail 0.9 mile over the hill into a wide meadow. At the bottom of the first steep hill, the Lookout Trail turns into the Yearling Trail where it intersects with Cage Creek Trail leading sharply left toward Crags Fire Road. Continue straight on the Yearling Trail, avoiding trails that lead to the left (14F). The State Park Maintenance Headquarters are clearly visible 1 mile ahead; go toward these buildings on the Yearling Trail.

The rocky and narrow trail ends at a gravel road near the park maintenance buildings (14G). Follow the road downhill 0.25 mile to the intersection of Mulholland Highway and Cornell Road. The trail continues just west of the northwest corner of the intersection (14H). Hop over a short, wooden fence and follow the trail northwest 0.25 mile into Paramount Ranch. At the bottom of the hill across a gravel parking area is the entrance to the western town where the television serial *Dr. Quinn, Medicine Woman* was filmed (14I). The detail that went into building this movie set makes it an interesting place to explore. Water and flush toilets are available here.

Take the dirt road (14J) back to the intersection of Mulholland Highway and Cornell Road (14H). From the intersection, follow the course back to

Malibu Creek State Park

the State Park Maintenance Headquarters and through the meadow. Stay on the main trail leading east, avoiding trails that veer off to the right, until you get to Cage Creek Trail. This trail is on the right just before the main trail leaves the meadow and goes uphill. A wooden post marks the intersection (14K). Turn right onto Cage Creek Trail, and descend 0.3 mile down a small canyon ending on Crags Fire Road near Malibu Creek (14L). Turn left and continue to the east on Crags Fire Road. The Lookout Trail (14E) taken on the way out is on the left; stay on Crags Fire Road to the right. Just beyond this, another short, dead-end trail on the right leads to the Century Reservoir. Continue straight up the hill and follow the same course taken on the way in. Watch carefully for the trail on the left just before the main road veers to the right at point 14C. Take the narrow trail that leads steeply up and over the short hill and back to Mulholland Highway (14B) and the parking area.

SIGNIFICANT TRAIL LANDMARKS

14A. Park near the corner of Mulholland Highway and Malibu Canyon Road or in the park.

14B. Trailhead on south side of Mulholland Highway through opening in fence.

14C. Turn right onto the High Road at intersection.

14D. Intersection with Crags Fire Road. Continue right on Crags Fire Road and begin to climb uphill.

14E. Intersection with the Lookout Trail. Turn right onto trail.

14F. Begin crossing a long meadow on the Yearling Trail.

14G. Park maintenance buildings. Trail ends at gravel road. Follow road downhill.

14H. Intersection of Mulholland Highway and Cornell Road. Trail continues on other side of the wooden fence near northwest corner of the intersection.

14I. Paramount Ranch.

14J. Dirt road leads back to Mulholland and Cornell intersection.

14K. Intersection with Cage Creek Trail. Turn right onto trail and head down into canyon to Crags Fire Road.

14L. Turn left and follow Crags Fire Road until it rejoins High Road. Return to the start the way you came.

15

Saddle Peak to Tapia Park

Distance: 7.25 miles

Course geometry: Point to point

Running time: 1–1.75 hours

Start altitude: 2,330 feet

Finish altitude: 480 feet

Elevation gain: 650 feet

Highest altitude: 2,600 feet

Difficulty: Easy

Water: None

Area management: California Department of Parks and Recreation
   Santa Monica Mountains Conservancy
   Mountains Restoration Trust
   Mountains Recreation and Conservation Authority

Maps: Malibu Beach (USGS)
   Trail Map of the Santa Monica Mountains, Central
   Trails Illustrated Santa Monica Mountains National Recreation Area

This downhill course begins at the summit of Saddle Peak overlooking the Pacific Ocean and descends into Cold Creek Preserve and the middle of Malibu Canyon. It follows one section of the Backbone Trail. The views of the mountains, valley, and Pacific Ocean along this course are phenomenal. For an extremely challenging workout, try running this course in reverse.

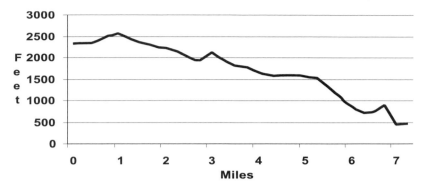

GETTING THERE

From the Ventura Freeway (Interstate 101), exit at Las Virgenes Road and drive south past the entrance to Tapia Park. Approximately 4.75 miles from the Ventura Freeway, immediately after crossing a bridge, turn right into a small parking lot. From Pacific Coast Highway take Malibu Canyon Road and turn left 1.6 miles after the tunnel into the small parking lot just before the bridge (H). Parking is $5. This is where the run will finish, so leave one car here.

To get to the start, take a second car and turn left out of the parking lot. Head north to Piuma Road and turn right. Drive on this winding road until it intersects with Schueren Road (off map) and turn left. Follow Schueren Road to the intersection of Saddle Peak Road and Stunt Road. Park on the shoulder of the north side of the large intersection (15A). The trail begins to the west.

THE RUN

From the intersection of Stunt Road and Schueren Road, the trailhead is approximately 300 feet down Stunt Road on the left (15A). The trail joins a steep, paved driveway, but when the driveway turns to the right, head up the dirt fire road and north around the fenced area with antennas (15B). Continue for 0.4 mile and, just before the trail takes a big turn to the left, look for a trail leading away to the right downhill (15C). Take this trail down a series of rocky switchbacks. In 1.8 miles, this trail joins the lower section of the Backbone Trail (watch for the sign). Take the Backbone Trail to the left (15D).

For the next 3.4 miles, the trail winds in and out of small canyons as it traverses the side of the mountain and crosses to Piuma Road. The trail picks up again to the left across Piuma Road (15E). Turn right onto the trail. The next 1.9 miles are through chaparral and woodlands punctuated with

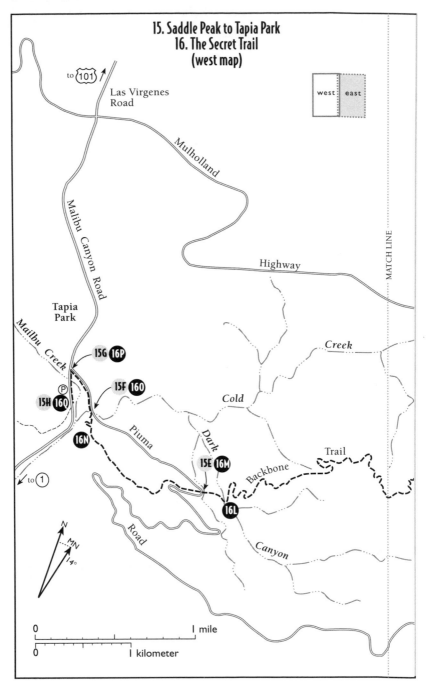

15. Saddle Peak to Tapia Park
16. The Secret Trail
(west map)

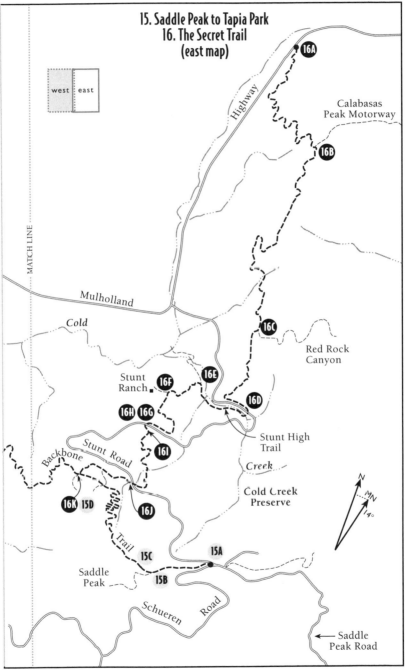

15. Saddle Peak to Tapia Park
16. The Secret Trail
(east map)

west : east

MATCH LINE

Highway

16A

Calabasas
Peak Motorway

16B

Mulholland

Cold

16C

Red Rock
Canyon

Stunt
Ranch

16F   **16E**

16D

16H **16G**

Stunt High
Trail

16I

Stunt Road

Backbone

Creek

Cold Creek
Preserve

16K **15D**

16J

N

MN
4°

Trail

15C   **15A**

Saddle
Peak

15B

Schueren   Road

← Saddle
Peak Road

Malibu Creek

moss-covered rocks. This wonderful section of the course is shaded under a thick canopy of oaks. The trail ends at Piuma Road after crossing a stream (15F). Follow Piuma Road to the left until it meets Malibu Canyon Road (15G). Turn left and run across the bridge on the left side, then cross over to the parking lot (15H).

SIGNIFICANT TRAIL LANDMARKS

15A. Trailhead on Stunt Road approximately 300 feet west of intersection.

15B. Follow dirt fire road around north side by the antennas.

15C. Turn right downhill.

15D. Turn left at intersection with the Backbone Trail.

15E. Cross Piuma Road and rejoin the trail to the left at the bend in the road. Turn right onto the trail.

15F. Trail ends at Piuma Road. Turn left and follow Piuma Road to Malibu Canyon Road.

15G. Turn left at Malibu Canyon Road and cross the bridge on the left side.

15H. Finish at the parking lot south of the bridge.

16
The Secret Trail

Distance: 12 miles
Course geometry: Point to point
Running time: 1.75–3.5 hours
Start altitude: 1,460 feet
Finish altitude: 480 feet
Elevation gain: 1,750 feet
Highest altitude: 2,150 feet
Difficulty: Moderate
Water: None
Area management· Mountains Restoration Trust
      California Department of Parks and Recreation
Maps: Malibu Beach (USGS)
      Trail Map of the Santa Monica Mountains, Central
      Trails Illustrated Santa Monica Mountains National Recreation Area

This meandering, point-to-point course is along ridges filled with beautiful rock formations and sweeping vistas. Many sections follow a lovely stream. This fabulous course has two big climbs and covers a lot of diverse territory in only 12 miles.

GETTING THERE

From the Ventura Freeway (Interstate 101), exit at Las Virgenes Road and drive south past the entrance to Tapia Park. Approximately 4.75 miles from

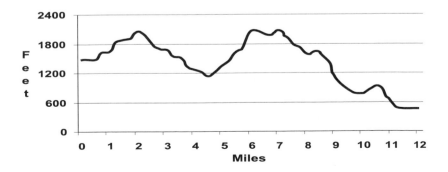

the Ventura Freeway, immediately after crossing a bridge, turn right into a small parking lot. From Pacific Coast Highway take Malibu Canyon Road and turn left 1.6 miles after the tunnel into the small parking lot just before the bridge (16H). Parking is $5. This is where the run will finish, so leave one car here.

To get to the start of the run, take a second car and turn left out of the parking lot. Drive north to Mulholland Highway, where you turn right. Go 1.8 miles past Stunt Road and look for a sign on the right marking the trailhead (16A). Parking is free in the dirt lot.

THE RUN

The trailhead is at the southeast end of the parking area (16A). The Secret Trail begins with many sharp turns with varied slopes and rocks. The trail joins the Calabasas Peak Motorway (16B) between two large rock formations. Turn right on Calabasas Peak Motorway and follow the main fire road south. Avoid the narrow trail on the right 100 feet from the turn. The fire road follows the ridge with views of several mountain ranges and colorful rock outcroppings. Climbing on these rocks is fun, but be careful.

The Red Rock Canyon Trail (16C) intersects from the left at the bottom of a long downhill section. There is a wooden bench located near the intersection with great views. Continue south on the Calabasas Peak Motorway. A short downhill section leads to Stunt Road (16D). Cross Stunt Road while watching carefully for cars and turn left. Two hundred yards to the east there is a chain-link fence with an opening. Portable toilets are located here. Take the narrow trail behind the fence leading down to the lower section of Cold Creek Canyon. This is the Stunt High Trail.

The Stunt High Trail follows a small stream through lush vegetation. Avoid any small trails leading to the left. The trail heads west for 0.6 mile and then turns south (left) away from the stream (16E). Avoid the trail 0.3 mile from the stream to the right leading to Stunt Ranch (16F), which is private property. In 1.2 miles the Stunt High Trail ends at a driveway. Cross the driveway and follow the opposite trail uphill to Stunt Road (16G). Turn right on Stunt Road and follow it uphill for about 0.1 mile (16H). Look for the continuation of the small, narrow Stunt High Trail (16I) on the left side of the road, 10 feet past the third power pole. Cautiously cross the street and follow the Stunt High Trail up 0.9 mile of switchbacks through sage scrub.

The Stunt High Trail ends again on Stunt Road (16J). Turn right on Stunt Road and in 150 yards watch for the Backbone Trail on the left side of the road. Cross the road, taking care to watch for cars, and follow this trail. Within 100 feet there is a small trail intersecting on the left. Avoid it and continue

The Secret Trail

to the right. At 0.2 mile, there is another intersection near a large oak tree (16K). Turn right towards the large red rocks and follow the gentle contours of the hillsides west. For the next 3.2 miles, the trail heads west over small ridges and down several switchbacks leading into Dark Canyon. Cross the stream and follow the trail uphill. Stay left at an intersection with a trail joining from the right (16L). This trail leads down to Piuma Road.

The Backbone Trail picks up again directly across Piuma Road and slightly to the left (16M); turn right onto the trail. The next 1.9 miles are through chaparral and woodlands punctuated with moss-covered rocks. This wonderful section is in shade under a thick canopy of oaks. Cross a paved driveway through a small meadow and continue straight ahead (16N). After crossing a stream, the trail ends at Piuma Road (16O). Follow Piuma Road to the left until it meets Malibu Canyon Road (16P). Turn left and go across the bridge on the left, then carefully cross to the parking lot (16Q).

SIGNIFICANT TRAIL LANDMARKS

16A. Trailhead at south end of parking area.

16B. Turn right onto Calabasas Peak Motorway.

16C. Intersection with Red Rock Canyon Road. Continue straight ahead.

16D. Cross Stunt Road. Continue easterly alongside the road 200 yards to an opening in the fence and turn onto the Stunt High Trail.

16E. Trail turns south (left) away from the stream.

16F. Intersection with trail to Stunt Ranch (off limits, private property). Continue on Stunt High Trail to the left.

16G. Cross driveway and follow trail uphill to Stunt Road.

16H. Turn right onto Stunt Road for short distance.

16I. Continuation of Stunt High Trail (I) on the left side of the road, 10 feet past the third power pole.

16J. At mile 6.4 turn right and cross the paved road heading downhill approximately 150 yards to the Backbone Trail on the left side of the road, then continue 3.4 miles farther to Piuma Road.

16K. At mile 6.6 at the intersection near a large oak tree, take the trail to the right toward the large red rocks.

16L. A small trail intersects from the right at mile 9.6. Continue straight ahead.

16M. Backbone Trail continues on the other side of Piuma Road.

16N. Cross paved driveway and continue straight ahead.

16O. At mile 11.7, cross the stream to trail's end at Piuma Road. Go left on road.

16P. Malibu Canyon Road. Turn left onto road and continue to your car at mile 12.

16Q. Parking lot.

Hondo Canyon

Distance: 6 miles

Course geometry: Point to point

Running time: 1–1.75 hours

Start altitude: 2,360 feet

Finish altitude: 870 feet

Elevation loss: 1,500 feet

Highest altitude: 2,440 feet

Difficulty: Easy

Water: None

Area management: California Department of Parks and Recreation
Mountains Restoration Trust

Maps: Topanga (USGS)
Trail Map of the Santa Monica Mountains, Central and West

This is a terrific downhill course offering you great views of Cold Creek Preserve, Malibu Canyon, Las Flores Canyon, and the Pacific Ocean. The trail passes by fossilized impressions of ancient shellfish in several large rocks. When the wildflowers are blooming, this course is fragrant and colorful.

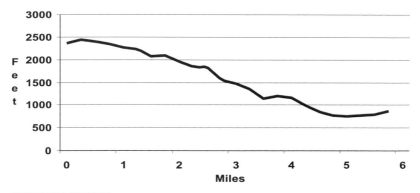

GETTING THERE

From Pacific Coast Highway, drive north on Topanga Canyon Boulevard 4.6 miles to Entrada Road and turn right. There is a small parking lot with water and toilets on the left about 50 yards up a steep hill. Parking is $3. From the San Fernando Valley take Topanga Canyon Boulevard south approximately 6 miles, turn left on Entrada Road, and drive up to the parking lot. This is where the run will finish, so leave one car here (17K).

To get to the start, return to Topanga Canyon Boulevard and turn left (south). After 0.9 mile, turn right at Fernwood Pacific Drive and follow the narrow twisting road through the hillside community of Fernwood. Drive uphill for 2.75 miles to where the road forks, and take the right fork to Saddle Peak Road. Continue for another 3.2 miles to the intersection of Saddle Peak Road, Schueren Road, and Stunt Road. Park on the wide shoulder on the right before the intersection.

THE RUN

From the trailhead on the east side of the parking area, head north up a gated, paved service road. The trail begins on your right about 25 yards up this service road at the second power pole (17A). The first 0.75 mile of the trail can be overgrown if there has been heavy rain in the winter and spring, so watch your step. At 0.5 mile from the start of the trail, look for a group of large boulders on the left side of the trail (17B). The fossil remains of shells in red-brown sedimentary rock are clearly visible here. These rocks were once at sea level, but now rest 2,000 feet above the ocean. Enjoy the fossils, but do not remove them.

Continue below the ridge for another 0.25 mile to where Hondo Canyon becomes visible as it drops down into Old Topanga Canyon. At 0.7 mile, a short trail to the right leads to Saddle Peak Road (17C). Take the trail to the left and continue down Hondo Canyon.

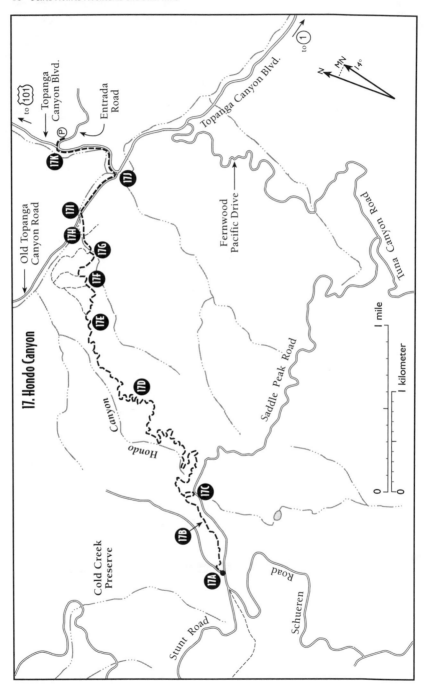

17. Hondo Canyon

The switchbacks alternate between warm and sunny and cool and shady. Watch for poison oak in the shaded areas. Tall runners should take extra care to avoid low-hanging branches in the wooded sections. Halfway down, the trail levels out in a heavily canopied area (17D). This is a peaceful place to stop and reflect on the surroundings. The next 2 miles descend gradually on the right side of the canyon into rolling hills covered with grass and flower-filled meadows (17E) and under beautiful coastal live oaks. The trail intersects with the Backbone Trail at mile 4.2 (17F) and again at mile 4.4 (17G). Continue

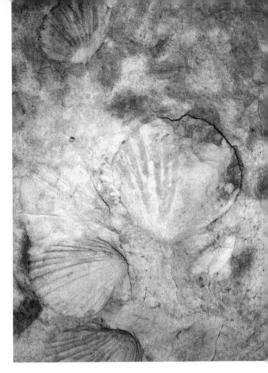

Shell fossils on Hondo Canyon Trail

to the right at both intersections. At mile 4.6, head left on the Backbone Trail (17H). The trail ends at Old Topanga Road (17I) after a stream crossing at mile 4.8. Turn right (south) and run 0.6 mile to Topanga Canyon Boulevard (17J). Turn left and run 0.5 mile to Entrada Road on the right. Proceed 50 yards up the hill to the parking lot (17K).

SIGNIFICANT TRAIL LANDMARKS

17A. Trail begins on right about 25 yards up paved service road at second power pole

17B. Large boulders with fossils.

17C. Turn left at mile 0.7 when coming within 200 feet of Saddle Peak Road.

17D. Tranquil, shaded area.

17E. Gradual descent through rolling hills.

17F. Intersection with Backbone Trail at mile 4.2. Stay to right.

17G. Second intersection with Backbone Trail at mile 4.4. Stay to right.

17H. Turn left at mile 4.6 onto the Backbone Trail.

17I. Old Topanga Road. Turn right onto paved road.

17J. Topanga Canyon Boulevard. Turn left to head toward Entrada Road.

17K. Parking lot.

18
Santa Ynez Canyon to Michael Lane

Distance: 9.5 miles
Course geometry: Loop
Running time: 1.5–2.3 hours
Start altitude: 600 feet
Finish altitude: 600 feet
Elevation gain: 1,400 feet
Highest altitude: 2,104 feet
Difficulty: Moderate
Water: Off course at Trippet Ranch
Area management: Topanga State Park
Maps: Topanga (USGS)
      Trail Map of the Santa Monica Mountains, East

This course begins in the cool Santa Ynez Canyon filled with large sycamores and oaks. In the summer months, the stream should be dry and easy to cross. The crossing can be more difficult during the rainy season, however. In the lower sections of the canyon, a lush canopy of foliage blocks direct sunlight. There are several areas where hearty patches of poison oak grow on both sides of the trail. You may need to slow down to avoid contact with it. A rugged climb up the Santa Ynez Canyon Trail will get your heart pumping. Panoramic views of both sides of the uniquely beautiful Santa Monica Mountains will elevate your spirits. The course ends with a 3-mile descent.

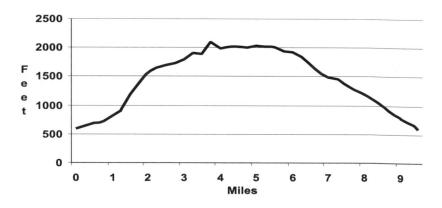

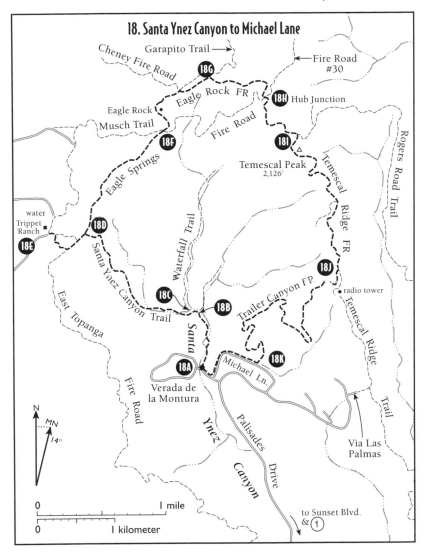

18. Santa Ynez Canyon to Michael Lane

GETTING THERE

From the Santa Monica Freeway (Interstate 10), drive north 4 miles on Pacific Coast Highway to Sunset Boulevard. Drive 0.3 mile east on Sunset Boulevard to Palisades Drive. Turn left onto Palisades Drive and continue up the hill for 2.4 miles. Turn left on Vereda de la Montura, passing Michael Lane on the right, and proceed down a short hill, which ends at the entrance to a gated residential area. Parking is available on either side of the street.

THE RUN

At the bottom of the hill, the trailhead (18A) is on the right behind a gate. The trail begins in a peaceful canyon filled with dense shrubs and trees growing along a small streambed. The trail crosses the streambed several times during the first mile. The trail is clearly visible; however, it occasionally branches off before rejoining the main trail. Follow the streambed and avoid right turns onto the Quarry Canyon Trail (18B), 0.4 mile from the start, and the Waterfall Trail (18C), 0.5 mile from the start. The Waterfall Trail is marked with a small sign and dead-ends 1.1 miles up the canyon.

An abrupt right turn and a climb onto a sunlit ridge marks the beginning of a 1-mile climb out of the canyon. From this ridge, you can see many mountains and sweeping views of the canyon. The trail winds through chaparral, climbing steadily around sandstone rock formations and tall brush with some steep sections. The trail ends at mile 2 on the Eagle Springs Fire Road (18D) with views overlooking Topanga Canyon and Santa Ynez Canyon. Trippet Ranch (18E) is located to the left about 0.5 mile down the fire road. Water and toilet facilities are available there if you need them, but that is not part of this run.

At the fire road, turn right and begin the 2.5-mile climb to Hub Junction. At mile 3, there is a fork in the fire road known as Eagle Junction (18F). The

Ferns along Santa Ynez Creek

narrow Musch Trail on the left leads down 2 miles to Trippet Ranch. The Eagle Springs Fire Road to the right leads 1.3 miles to Hub Junction. Take the Eagle Rock Fire Road on the left, which also leads to Hub Junction in 1.3 miles. Watch for signs indicating Eagle Rock on the right.

After a steep, 0.5-mile climb from Eagle Junction, you reach the highest point (18G) on the course, elevation 2,104 feet. Pause to catch your breath and enjoy the excellent views of the many mountain ranges that surround the Los Angeles Basin.

Continue east 0.8 mile on the fire road to Hub Junction (18H). Hub Junction is the junction of four major fire roads, which connect like spokes in a giant wheel. Hub Junction is a good spot to take a break or meet friends.

From Hub Junction, take the Temescal Ridge Fire Road south. Enjoy the relatively flat trail as it follows the ridge back toward the Pacific Ocean. On the left, 0.5 mile from Hub Junction, a fork in the trail leads to Will Rogers State Historic Park (18I). Continue to the right on the fire road until mile 6.1 (18J) where the road forks again. Take the Trailer Canyon Fire Road to the right where a sign directs you to Michael Lane.

The next 3.4 miles are all downhill. Views of Los Angeles, Santa Monica, Pacific Palisades, and the ocean are often spectacular, but watch your footing on the loose gravel. The fire road ends on Michael Lane (18K), a paved residential road. Turn right and run 0.7 mile downhill to Vereda de la Montura. Turn right to return to the start.

SIGNIFICANT TRAIL LANDMARKS

18A. Trailhead at bottom of hill on the right behind gate.

18B. Quarry Canyon Trail on the right. Continue straight ahead.

18C. Waterfall Trail on the right. Continue straight ahead.

18D. Trail ends at Eagle Springs Fire Road at mile 2. Turn right onto road.

18E. Trippet Ranch with water and toilet facilities (not part of this course).

18F. Eagle Junction—intersection of Musch Trail and Eagle Springs and Eagle Rock Fire Roads.

18G. Highest point on the course, 2,104 feet.

18H. Hub Junction at mile 4.3.

18I. Fork in trail. Trail on the left leads to Will Rogers State Historic Park. Continue to the right.

18J. At fork, turn right onto Trailer Canyon Fire Road.

18K. Michael Lane, a paved road. Turn right onto road, run 0.7 mile to Vereda de la Montura, and turn right to return to the start.

19

Santa Ynez Canyon to Will Rogers State Historic Park

Distance: 11.25 miles
Course geometry: Point to point
Running time: 1.5–3 hours
Start altitude: 600 feet
Finish altitude: 420 feet
Elevation gain: 1,500 feet
Highest altitude: 2,104 feet
Difficulty: Moderate
Water: Off course at Trippet Ranch and at the finish
Area management: Topanga State Park
Maps: Topanga (USGS)
      Trail Map of the Santa Monica Mountains, East

This run starts in a beautiful, cool canyon and continues across ridges with huge mountain and coastal views. This scenic run is challenging and can be hot, so be prepared. Will Rogers State Historic Park has water, restrooms, and a nice grass field for relaxing. Explore the home of cowboy, actor, and humorist Will Rogers and, if you are lucky, watch a polo game.

GETTING THERE

From the San Diego Freeway (Interstate 405), take Sunset Boulevard west. After winding through Brentwood, you arrive in Pacific Palisades where the park is located, approximately 4.6 miles from the San Diego Freeway. Watch for the park sign and turn right on Will Rogers Road. Drive up to the top of the

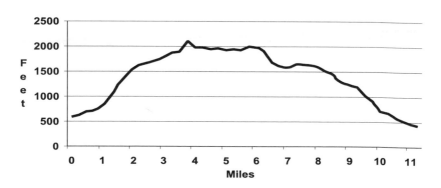

hill. If the parking lot gate is closed, park the car on a non-posted residential street south of the park entrance. If the park is open, leave the car in the parking lot. Parking is $5. This is where the run will finish, so leave one car here.

From Will Rogers State Historic Park, take the second car and return to Sunset Boulevard, where you will turn right (west). Proceed 3.4 miles and turn right on Palisades Drive. Continue up the hill for 2 miles and turn left on Vereda de la Montura. Proceed down a short hill that ends at a gated residential area. Park on either side of Vereda de la Montura.

THE RUN

At the bottom of the hill, the trailhead (19A) is on the right behind a gate. The trail begins in a peaceful canyon filled with dense shrubs and trees growing along a small streambed. The trail crosses the streambed several times in the first mile. Trail visibility is good, although there are some areas where it branches off before rejoining the main trail. Follow the streambed and avoid right turns onto the Quarry Canyon Trail (19B), 0.4 mile from the start, and the Waterfall Trail (19C), 0.5 mile from the start. The Waterfall Trail, which dead-ends 1.1 miles up the canyon, is marked with a small sign.

The stream is often dry during the summer months, but crossing may require a little more effort during rainy weather. In the lower sections of the canyon, a lush canopy of foliage blocks direct sunlight. Watch for hearty patches of poison oak adjacent to the trail.

An abrupt right turn and a climb onto a sunlit ridge marks the beginning of a 1-mile climb out of the canyon to a ridge. From here, you see mountains in all directions, including views of the canyon you just passed through. The trail winds through chaparral, climbing steadily around sandstone rock formations and tall brush with some steep sections. The trail ends at mile 2 on the Eagle Springs Fire Road (19D) with views overlooking Topanga Canyon to the west and Santa Ynez Canyon to the southeast. Trippet Ranch (19E) is located to the left about 0.5 mile down the fire road. Water and toilet facilities are available there if you need them, but that is not part of this course.

Turn right onto Eagle Springs Fire Road and begin the 2.5-mile climb to Hub Junction. At mile 3, a four-way intersection is known as Eagle Junction (19F). The narrow Musch Trail on the left leads to Trippet Ranch. Eagle Springs Fire Road to the right leads to Hub Junction. Straight ahead from the direction you came, the Eagle Rock Fire Road also leads to Hub Junction in 1.3 miles. Take this fire road. Watch for signs indicating Eagle Rock on the right. Pause to catch your breath and enjoy the excellent views of the many mountain ranges that surround the Los Angeles Basin. After a steep, 0.5-mile

19. Santa Ynez Canyon to Will Rogers State Historic Park

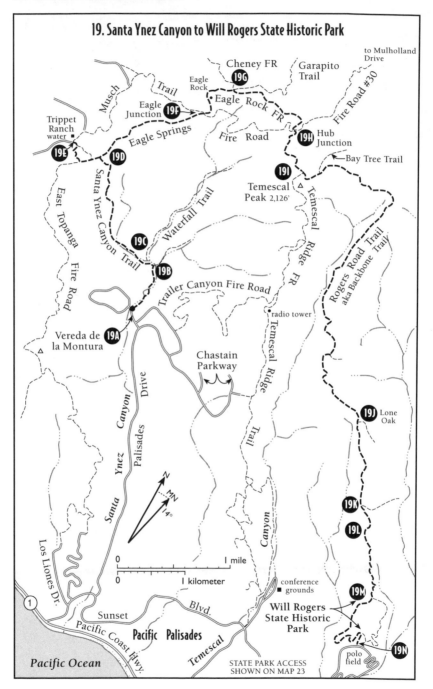

Trail above Will Rogers State Historic Park (Photo by Debbie Bradford)

climb from Eagle Junction you will reach the highest point (19G) on the course, elevation 2,104 feet.

Continue east on the fire road 0.8 mile to Hub Junction (19H). Hub Junction is the junction of four major fire roads, which connect like spokes in a giant wheel. Hub Junction is a good spot to take a break or meet friends.

From Hub Junction, take the Temescal Ridge Fire Road that leads south (straight ahead from the direction you arrived). With most of the uphill sections behind you, enjoy the ridge heading back toward the Pacific Ocean.

At 0.5 mile from Hub Junction, Rogers Road Trail (19I) leading to Will Rogers State Historic Park emerges on the left with a sign indicating 6 miles. Turn left onto the trail, which starts in an easterly direction with a short descent over a rocky section that is subject to occasional landslides from the steep hill on the right. In the spring and early summer months, the trail is bright with orange, violet, red, and yellow wildflowers. The shaded areas may have poison oak. The trail winds its way to a lone oak (19J) 3 miles from the Will Rogers State Historic Park.

At the lone oak, you can look northeast into upper Rustic Canyon and east to the Sullivan Ridge Fire Road that runs along the ridge. The trail descends south from the lone oak over rocky terrain.

Watch for a narrow trail to the left leading down into Rustic Canyon (19K). Do not take this trail. Continue south on the main trail. The final descent is steep and short portions may require walking, especially if there are hikers or cyclists in the area. The trail leads to a small bridge high above the canyon (19L), then drops to a fire road (19M) that encircles Will Rogers State Historic Park. Turn right onto the fire road and follow it to the parking lot, where you will find water and toilet facilities (19N). Go west on the paved road downhill to your car.

SIGNIFICANT TRAIL LANDMARKS

19A. Trailhead at bottom of hill on the right behind gate.

19B. Quarry Canyon Trail on the right. Continue straight ahead.

19C. Waterfall Trail on the right. Continue straight ahead.

19D. Trail ends at Eagle Springs Fire Road. Turn right onto road.

19E. Trippet Ranch 0.5 mile to the left (not part of this course).

19F. Eagle Junction—intersection of Musch Trail and Eagle Springs and Eagle Rock Fire Roads. Follow Eagle Rock Fire Road north.

19G. Highest point on the course.

19H. Hub Junction at mile 4.3. Follow Temescal Ridge Fire Road south.

19I. Left turn onto Rogers Road Trail.

19J. Lone oak tree.

19K. Narrow trail to the left leading to Rustic Canyon. Continue south on main trail.

19L. Bridge above canyon.

19M. Fire road around Will Rogers State Historic Park. Turn right onto road.

19N. Parking lot. Go west downhill to your car.

20
Santa Ynez Canyon to Los Liones Canyon

Distance: 7.6 miles

Course geometry: Point to point

Running time: 1.25–2 hours

Start altitude: 600 feet

Finish altitude: 200 feet

Elevation gain: 1,800 feet

Highest altitude: 1,575 feet

Difficulty: Moderate

Water: Off course at Trippet Ranch

Area management: Topanga State Park

Maps: Topanga (USGS)
   Trail Map of the Santa Monica Mountains, East

This point-to-point course begins in a splendid canyon with numerous stream crossings. Heavy foliage makes this area cool and crisp in the early mornings. The canyon trail joins the East Topanga Fire Road and leads to Los Liones Canyon, featuring splendid views, dense foliage, and ivy-covered trees.

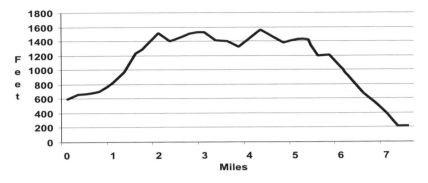

An optional 1-mile side trip to the Parker Mesa Overlook rewards you with a 360-degree view of Los Angeles and the Pacific Ocean, making you feel like you are hovering in a helicopter.

GETTING THERE

From the Santa Monica Freeway (Interstate 10), drive north 4 miles on Pacific Coast Highway to Sunset Boulevard. Drive east on Sunset Boulevard 0.2 mile to Los Liones Drive and turn left. Drive 0.4 mile to where the road ends. This is where the run will finish, so leave one car here in the smaller parking area to the right. The larger parking lot on the left belongs to the church.

With the second car, return to Sunset Boulevard, turn left, and drive 0.2 mile east to Palisades Drive. Turn left on Palisades Drive and continue uphill for 2 miles. Turn left on Vereda de la Montura and drive past Michael Lane on the right. Proceed down a short hill that ends at the entrance to a gated residential area. Park on either side of Vereda de la Montura.

THE RUN

The trailhead (20A) is on the right behind a gate at the bottom of the hill. The trail begins in a peaceful canyon filled with dense shrubs and trees along a small streambed. The trail crosses the streambed several times for the first mile. Trail visibility is good, although there are some areas where it branches off before rejoining the main trail. Follow the streambed and avoid right turns onto the Quarry Canyon Trail (20B), 0.4 mile from the start, and the Waterfall Trail (20C), 0.5 mile from the start. The Waterfall Trail, which dead-ends 1.1 miles up the canyon, is marked with a small sign.

The stream is often dry during the summer months, but crossing may require a little more effort during rainy weather. In the lower sections of the canyon, a lush canopy of foliage blocks direct sunlight. Watch for hearty patches of poison oak adjacent to the trail.

An abrupt right turn and a climb onto a sunlit ridge marks the beginning of a 1-mile climb out of the canyon. From this ridge, you see mountains in all directions, including views of the canyon you just passed through. The

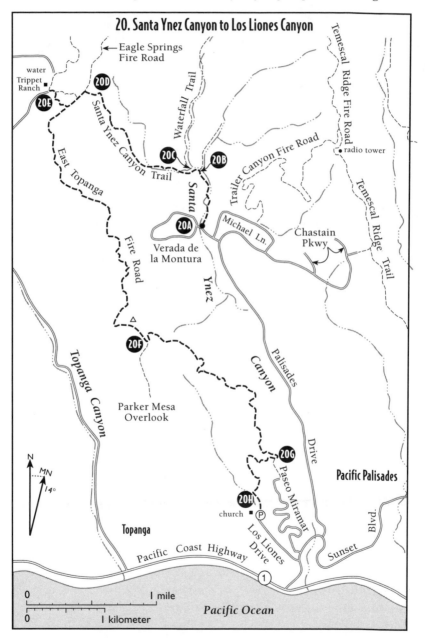

20. Santa Ynez Canyon to Los Liones Canyon

View from Parker Mesa Overlook

trail winds through chaparral, climbing steadily around sandstone rock formations and tall brush with some steep sections. The trail ends at mile 2 on the Eagle Springs Fire Road (20D) with views overlooking Topanga Canyon and Santa Ynez Canyon.

Turn left on the fire road and run downhill. Notice the signs marking two narrow trails leading to Trippet Ranch on the right. The fire road forks at the bottom of a short hill. Take the left fork heading west on the East Topanga Fire Road. The right fork leads to the Trippet Ranch (20E). Water and toilet facilities are available there if you need them, but that is not part of this course.

Climb on the fire road for the next 2.5 miles to where the Parker Mesa Overlook Trail joins the fire road on the right (20F). This 0.5-mile trail is worth the extra effort as it leads to a wide ridge with spectacular, unobstructed views of Pacific Palisades, Santa Monica, and much of the Los Angeles Basin. From the Parker Mesa Overlook, return to the fire road and turn right.

Continue for 1.9 miles and at the bottom of a long, steep section watch closely for a right turn onto the narrow Los Liones Trail (20G). The intersection connects at a sharp angle, so slow down since too much momentum tends to take you past it. Marked with a sign, the Los Liones Canyon Trail takes a serpentine course along the contours of the chaparral-covered hills. The lower section of the 1.5-mile trail has tiny canyons filled with lush vegetation and ivy-covered trees. The trail ends at Los Liones Drive (20H).

SIGNIFICANT TRAIL LANDMARKS

20A. Trailhead at bottom of hill on the right behind gate.

20B. Quarry Canyon Trail on the right. Continue straight ahead.

20C. Waterfall Trail on the right. Continue straight ahead.

20D. Trail ends at Eagle Springs Fire Road at mile 2. Turn right onto road.

20E. Trippet Ranch with water and toilet facilities (not part of this course).

20F. Intersection with Parker Mesa Overlook Trail on the right.

20G. Right turn onto Los Liones Canyon Trail, which intersects from a sharp angle at the bottom of a steep hill.

20H. Trail ends at Los Liones Drive.

21
Palisades Highlands to Trippet Ranch Loop

Distance: 13.1 miles

Course geometry: Out-and-back loop

Running time: 1.75–3.25 hours

Start altitude: 1,570 feet

Finish altitude: 1,570 feet

Elevation gain: 2,200 feet

Highest altitude: 2,070 feet

Difficulty: Strenuous

Water: At start, finish, and points (21J) and (21L)

Area management: Topanga State Park

Maps: Topanga (USGS)
   Trail Map of the Santa Monica Mountains, East

This challenging run has several climbs guaranteed to get your heart pumping. The course meanders along ridges and into canyons and has a variety of enjoyable views. Water is at the start and finish and at miles 6.4 and 7.4 near Trippet Ranch. Toilets are at the start and at Trippet Ranch.

GETTING THERE

From the San Diego Freeway (Interstate 405), take Sunset Boulevard west 8 miles to Palisades Drive and turn right. Follow Palisades Drive 3.9 miles until you reach Via Las Palmas. Turn right through the gate. Drive straight uphill across the circular driveway and up the access road. You will see a small parking lot 50 feet up this road on your left. Park here or on the side of the

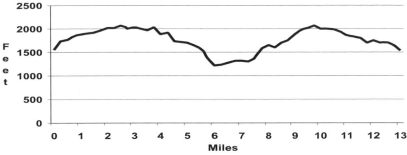

access road. The parking lot has drinking water and flush toilets. Should you choose to park at Trippet Ranch (21J) and run from there, note that the parking lot closes at sunset.

THE RUN

The trailhead (21A) begins at the concrete drainage culvert across from the parking lot entrance. The first 400 yards are up a short hill along the concrete drainage culvert leading to Temescal Ridge Trail (21B). You can immediately appreciate the view of the mountains, the Pacific Ocean, and the Mediterranean-style homes clustered together in the valley below. Turn left onto Temescal Ridge Trail and climb a short hill leading to a ridge. It is common to see rabbits, snakes, mice, beetles, spiders, and birds as you climb the 3 miles to the Rogers Road Trail.

After 1.4 miles, you will pass Trailer Canyon Fire Road (21C), which descends to the left. Stay to the right and continue for another 1.6 miles past the Rogers Road Trail (21D) that connects from the right at the bottom of a short downhill section. Continue on the fire road for another 0.5 mile to Hub Junction where four fire roads converge (21E). The bulletin board here is a great location to rest or to meet friends. Just before you reach Hub Junction, there are several large rock formations on the right with exquisite views.

From Hub Junction, turn left (west) up a short, steep hill onto Eagle Rock Fire Road. The San Fernando Valley below extends to the distant mountains. Eagle Rock is on the left 1 mile from Hub Junction. A sign marks a short trail to the south-facing rock overlooking Santa Ynez Canyon. The highest point on the course (21F) is just before a steep and rocky, 0.5-mile downhill section to Eagle Junction (21G), the intersection with the Musch Trail and Eagle Springs Fire Road (Eagle Junction).

The Musch Trail joins from the right and Eagles Springs Fire Road is on the left leading to the east. Continue straight 1 mile downhill passing Santa

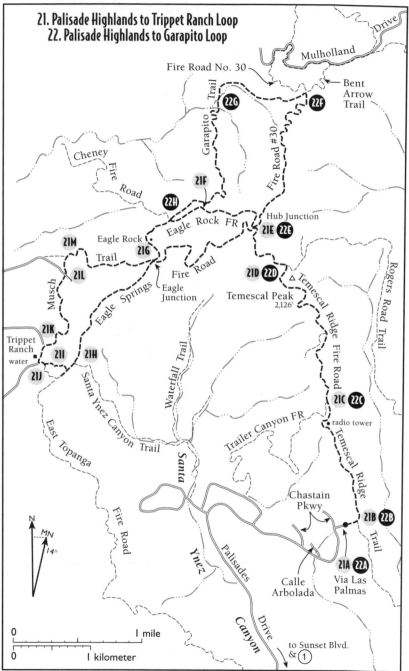

21. Palisade Highlands to Trippet Ranch Loop
22. Palisade Highlands to Garapito Loop

Temescal Ridge Trail

Ynez Canyon Trail on the left (21H). Follow the fire road as it curves to the right in 0.1 mile and turn right where a sign marks the Nature Trail (21I). This trail goes through a grove of oak trees and leads to the Trippet Ranch parking lot, which has water and toilet facilities.

Continue on the paved road located at the northeast corner of the parking lot near the bulletin board. The Musch Trail (21J) is about 400 yards from the parking lot on the right (21K). Turn right onto the trail. One mile from the parking lot, the Musch Trail crosses another paved road near a small campground (21L). The trail continues to the right of the water fountain along a split-rail fence and galvanized-pipe horse corral. Continue on the main trail through an open meadow (21M), staying to the right on Musch Trail at a fork from the left. Musch Trail ascends steeply uphill to Eagle Junction (21G).

Back at Eagle Junction, turn left onto Eagle Springs Fire Road. This leads to Hub Junction (21E). Turn right at Hub Junction and run south on the Temescal Ridge Trail. Watch for the radio tower that marks the intersection with Trailer Canyon Fire Road (21C). At the junction, stay to the left on the Temescal Ridge Trail to return to the start.

SIGNIFICANT TRAIL LANDMARKS

21A. Trailhead across from the parking lot entrance.

21B. Left turn onto Temescal Ridge Trail.

21C. Junction with Trailer Canyon Fire Road on the left. Stay to the right.

21D. Junction with Rogers Road Trail on the right. Stay on the fire road.

21E. Hub Junction at mile 3.3. Turn left (west) up a short, steep hill onto Eagle Rock Fire Road.

21F. High point on the course, 2,070 feet.

21G. Eagle Junction.

21H. Intersection of Santa Ynez Canyon Trail. Continue on the fire road.

21I. Right turn onto the Nature Trail leading to Trippet Ranch.

21J. Musch Trail.

21K. Right turn onto Musch Trail from the paved road 400 yards from parking lot.

21L. Cross paved road near campground. Trail continues to the right of the water fountain. Stay on Musch Trail to Eagle Junction.

21M. Meadow. Stay right at a fork from the left. At Eagle Junction, turn left onto Eagle Springs Fire Road to return to Hub Junction. Retrace route back to the start.

22
Palisades Highlands to Garapito Loop

Distance: 11.5 miles

Course geometry: Out-and-back loop

Running time: 1.75–3 hours

Start altitude: 1,570 feet

Finish altitude: 1,570 feet

Elevation gain: 1,800 feet

Highest altitude: 2,070 feet

Difficulty: Moderate

Water: At the start and finish

Area management: Topanga State Park

Maps: Topanga (USGS)

Trail Map of the Santa Monica Mountains, East

This course features a challenging climb on a fire road leading to Hub Junction and a loop on the lovely Garapito Trail. A wonderful secluded canyon and majestic views from ridges should satisfy everyone.

GETTING THERE

From the San Diego Freeway (Interstate 405), drive west 8 miles on Sunset Boulevard to Palisades Drive. Turn right and follow Palisades Drive 3.9 miles until you reach Via Las Palmas. Turn right through the gate. Drive straight uphill across the circular driveway and up the access road. You will see a small

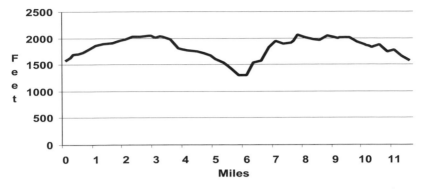

parking lot 50 feet up this road on your left. Park here or on the side of the access road. The parking lot has drinking water and flush toilets.

THE RUN

The trail begins at a concrete drainage culvert across from the parking lot entrance (22A) and continues 400 yards up a short hill leading to the Temescal Ridge Trail (22B). You can immediately enjoy the views of the mountains, the Pacific Ocean, and the Mediterranean-style homes clustered together in the valley below. Turn left on the Temescal Ridge Trail and climb a short hill leading to a ridge. The trail follows the ridge between Temescal Canyon and Santa Ynez Canyon. It is common to see rabbits, snakes, mice, beetles, spiders, and birds as you climb the 3 miles to the intersection with the Rogers Road Trail.

At 1.4 miles from the start, pass the Trailer Canyon Fire Road (22C), which descends to the left. Stay to the right and continue running for another 1.6 miles past the trailhead of the Will Rogers Trail (22D) located on the right at the bottom of a short downhill section. Continue on the fire road for another 0.5 mile to Hub Junction (22E), where four fire roads converge. This is a great location to meet friends. Just before you reach Hub Junction, there are several large rock formations on the right with appealing views.

From Hub Junction, head northeast (right) downhill on Fire Road No. 30. At 1.75 miles beyond Hub Junction, a wide left turn marks an intersection with the Bent Arrow Trail on the right and the Garapito Trail (22F) on the left. The fire road continues uphill to the left beyond the Garapito Trail. Turn left onto the Garapito Trail. Although cyclists are barred from using this trail, proceed with caution.

The Garapito Trail descends into the canyon and soon parallels a small stream as it drops steadily. Follow the gentle contours of the hillsides through chaparral and sagebrush. At the bottom of the canyon, the trail crosses a stream under a large oak tree (22G). On the other side of the stream, follow the trail to

the left (south) and begin the climb back up through a series of long switch-backs through chaparral. Watch for low-hanging branches along these sections.

Just before reaching the Eagle Rock Fire Road, the trail turns west (22H). At the fire road, turn left (east) and return to Hub Junction on the Eagle Rock Fire Road. At Hub Junction, turn right and return to the start the same way you came.

SIGNIFICANT TRAIL LANDMARKS

22A. Trailhead across from the parking lot entrance.

22B. Left turn onto Temescal Ridge Trail.

22C. Junction with Trailer Canyon Fire Road on the left. Stay to the right.

22D. Junction with Rogers Road Trail on the right. Stay on the fire road.

22E. Hub Junction. Head northeast downhill on Fire Road No. 30.

22F. Four-way intersection. Turn left onto Garapito Trail.

22G. Stream crossing. On opposite side, follow trail to the left and head uphill.

22H. Turn left onto Eagle Rock Fire Road and return to Hub Junction (22E). From here, return to the start the same way you came.

23
Palisades Highlands to Will Rogers State Historic Park

Distance: 9.4 miles

Course geometry: Point to point

Running time: 1.25–2.5 hours

Start altitude: 1,570 feet

Finish altitude: 420 feet

Elevation gain: 600 feet

Highest altitude: 2,070 feet

Difficulty: Moderate

Water: At the start and finish

Area management: Topanga State Park

Maps: Topanga (USGS)
Trail Map of the Santa Monica Mountains, East

This is a wide and popular trail shared with equestrians, hikers, and cyclists. The run starts with a challenging climb on a fire road and a 6-mile run over

Grassy hillside trail

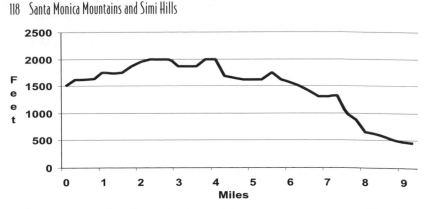

rocky terrain. It offers fantastic views of the mountains, ocean, and Los Angeles. On clear days, you can see Catalina Island and the distant San Gabriel and San Bernardino Mountains. Hot weather should encourage an early start, as there is no water on the course and much of it is on exposed ridges.

GETTING THERE

From the San Diego Freeway (Interstate 405), take Sunset Boulevard west 4.6 miles. Turn right onto Will Rogers Road and drive to the top of the hill. If the parking lot gate is closed, park the car on a non-posted residential street below the park entrance. If the park is open, leave the car in the parking lot for a $5 fee. This is where the run will finish, so leave one car here.

From Will Rogers State Historic Park, take the other car and return down the hill to a right turn (west) onto Sunset Boulevard. Proceed 3.4 miles to Palisades Drive and turn right. Follow Palisades Drive 3.9 miles until you reach Via Las Palmas and turn right through the gates. Drive straight uphill across a circular driveway and up the access road. Fifty feet up this road you will see a small parking lot on your left. Park here or on the side of the access road. Parking is free. The parking lot has flush toilets and drinking water.

THE RUN

The trail begins (23A) at a concrete drainage culvert across from the parking lot entrance and continues 400 yards up a short hill leading to the Temescal Ridge Trail (23B). You can immediately appreciate the views of the mountains, the Pacific Ocean, and the Mediterranean-style homes clustered in the valley below. Turn left onto Temescal Ridge Trail (23B) and climb a short hill leading to a ridge. The course follows the ridge between Temescal Canyon on the right and Santa Ynez Canyon on the left. It is common to see rabbits, snakes, mice, beetles, spiders, and birds as you climb the 3 miles to the Rogers Road Trail.

23. Palisade Highlands to Will Rogers State Historic Park

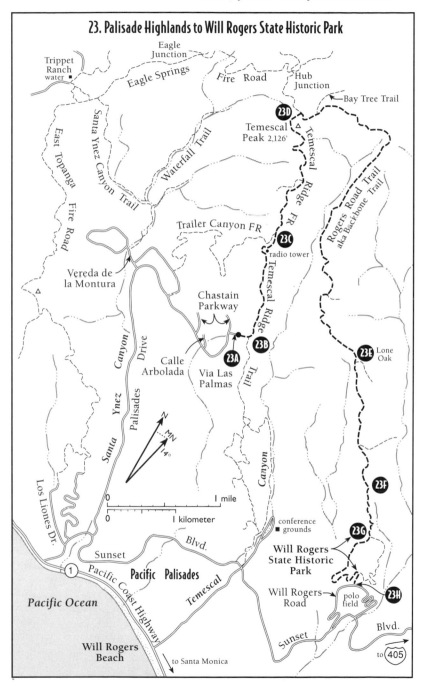

Eagle Junction

Trippet Ranch water ■

Eagle Springs

Fire Road

Hub Junction

Bay Tree Trail

East Topanga Fire Road

Santa Ynez Canyon Trail

Waterfall Trail

23D

Temescal Peak 2,126'

Temescal Ridge FR

Rogers Road Trail aka Backbone Trail

Trailer Canyon FR

23C

radio tower

Vereda de la Montura

△

Chastain Parkway

Temescal Ridge Trail

23B

23E Lone Oak

Canyon Drive

Calle Arbolada

Via Las Palmas

23A

N

MN 14°

Palisades

Santa Ynez

Canyon

23F

0   1 mile

0   1 kilometer

conference ■ grounds

23G

Will Rogers State Historic Park

Los Liones Dr.

Blvd.

Sunset

1

Pacific Coast Highway

Pacific   Palisades

Temescal

Will Rogers Road

polo field

23H

Pacific Ocean

Blvd.

Sunset

to **405**

Will Rogers Beach

to Santa Monica

At 1.4 miles from the start, pass Trailer Canyon Fire Road (23C), which descends to the left. Stay to the right and continue running for another 1.6 miles to the trailhead of the Rogers Road Trail (23D) located on the right at the bottom of a short downhill section. A marker at this junction indicates it is 6 miles to Will Rogers State Historic Park. The trail begins with a short descent over a rocky trail that is subject to occasional landslides from the steep hill on the right. During the spring and early summer months, the trail is bright with orange, violet, red, and yellow wildflowers. Watch out for poison oak in the more shaded areas. The trail winds it way to a solitary oak tree (23E) located 3 miles from the Will Rogers State Historic Park.

At the lone oak, you can look east into Rustic Canyon and across to Sullivan Ridge. The trail descends south from the lone oak over rocky terrain. The final descent is steep and short portions may require walking, especially if there are many hikers or cyclists. The trail leads to a small bridge high above the canyon (23F) and then to a fire road (23G) that encircles Will Rogers State Historic Park. Turn right onto the fire road and return to the parking lot where you will find water and toilet facilities (23H). Continue west downhill to your car.

Option: If only one car is available, you can run this course in either direction as an out-and-back run.

SIGNIFICANT TRAIL LANDMARKS
    23A. Trailhead across from the parking lot entrance.
    23B. Turn left onto Temescal Ridge Trail.
    23C. Junction with Trailer Canyon Fire Road on the left. Stay to the right.
    23D. Junction with Rogers Road Trail. Turn right onto the trail.
    23E. A solitary oak tree. Trail descends south.

The Lone Oak on the Rogers Road Trail

23F. Bridge high above canyon.

23G. Fire road around Will Rogers State Historic Park. Turn right onto fire road to return to the parking lot.

23H. Restrooms and water facilities. Continue west downhill to your car.

24
Temescal Canyon Loop

Distance: 3.5 miles
Course geometry: Loop
Running time: 0.5–1 hour
Start altitude: 300 feet
Finish altitude: 300 feet
Elevation gain: 1,160 feet
Highest altitude: 1,160 feet
Difficulty: Easy
Water: At trailhead
Area management: California State Parks
    Santa Monica Mountains Conservancy
    Mountains Recreation and Conservation Authority
Maps: Topanga (USGS)
    Trail Map of the Santa Monica Mountains, East

This popular trail is only 1 mile from the ocean, so you can run on the beach and in the mountains on the same visit. With easy access to the trailhead, you don't need a lot of spare time to enjoy the short, steep loops through riparian canyons and chaparral-covered ridges.

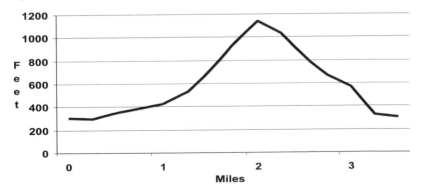

GETTING THERE

From the San Diego Freeway (Interstate 405), drive west on Sunset Boulevard 6 miles to Temescal Canyon Road. Turn right and park in the parking lot for $6. If the parking lot is closed, go south on Temescal Canyon Road and park on either side of the street (watch for posted parking restrictions). Walk north on Temescal and cross Sunset Boulevard to the parking lot. If you are come from Pacific Coast Highway, drive up Temescal Canyon Road 1 mile to the parking area. Cars must be out of the parking lot by sunset.

THE RUN

The trailhead (24A) is to the left of the restrooms located at the north end of the parking lot. The trail drops down a short hill and crosses a small bridge

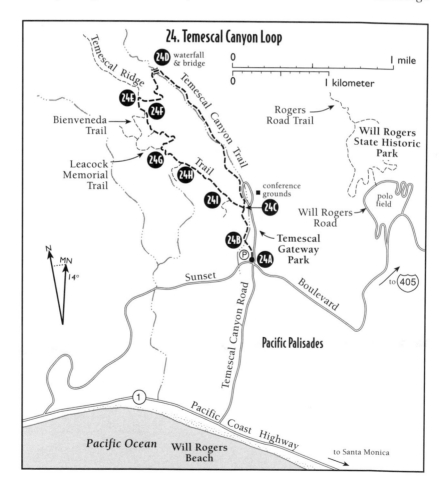

24. Temescal Canyon Loop

Temescal Canyon

over a stream (24B). Turn right and continue north into the canyon. Initially, the trail follows the left side of the canyon above a small creek through lush vegetation of ground cover, shrubs, and oak trees. In season, wildflowers carpet the hillside with brilliant colors. Some sections of the trail are surrounded by dense chaparral canopies that form cool, dark tunnels. Listen for the peaceful sounds of the stream.

Continue straight ahead at a four-way intersection (24C), following the trail markers to the waterfall 1 mile from the start. There is another bridge over a large pool beneath a 15-foot waterfall (24D). Hikers often congregate on the rocks that surround this tranquil place.

After leaving the waterfall, the trail climbs steeply out of the canyon. Nearly 0.35 mile from the waterfall is a trail junction (24E). If you desire additional mileage, continue uphill to the right and turn back when desired. Otherwise, turn sharply left following the trail 1.8 miles back to the start.

Keep to the left, continuing down the canyon whenever you encounter other trails. When the Bienveneda Trail intersects from the right (24F), you continue left. When the Leacock Memorial Trail (24G) intersects from the right shortly thereafter, you continue left. At a high point (24H), take the trail to the left. A short distance farther, a narrow trail leads off to the right toward houses (24I); do not take this trail. Stay left and continue downhill. Turn right at the bottom of the canyon, and return to the start.

SIGNIFICANT TRAIL LANDMARKS

24A. Trailhead left of restrooms at north end of parking lot.

24B. Turn right after bridge.

24C. Four-way intersection. Continue straight ahead to the waterfall.

24D. Bridge near waterfall.

24E. Trail junction. Make an abrupt left turn and continue uphill. Turn right if extra mileage is desired.

24F. Bienveneda Trail intersects from the right; continue to the left.

24G. Leacock Memorial Trail intersects from the right; continue to the left.

24H. High point; continue to the left.

24I. Narrow trail to the right toward houses; stay left and continue downhill.

25

Westridge to Temescal Canyon

Distance: 13.75 miles

Course geometry: Point to point

Running time: 2–3.5 hours

Start altitude: 1,260 feet

Finish altitude: 300 feet

Elevation gain: 1,700 feet

Highest altitude: 2,040 feet

Difficulty: Moderate

Water: At point 25B and the finish

Area management: California State Parks
 Santa Monica Mountains Conservancy
 Mountains Recreation and Conservation Authority
 Los Angeles County Sanitation

Maps: Topanga (USGS)
 Trail Map of the Santa Monica Mountains, East

This course run provides majestic views of Los Angeles, the Pacific Ocean, and the San Fernando Valley. It begins with a moderate climb for 3.7 miles on a fire road. Several sections include trails that parallel the fire road, providing an interesting blend of terrain and vegetation. The final mile follows a small stream through lush vegetation ending at Temescal Gateway Park, where there are picnic tables, restrooms, and water.

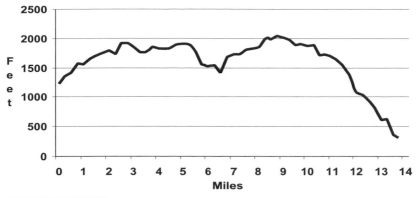

GETTING THERE

From Pacific Coast Highway, turn north on Temescal Canyon Road. Cross Sunset Boulevard and park one car in the parking lot on the left. Parking is $6. This is where the run will finish. Parking is also available south of Sunset Boulevard on Temescal Canyon Road.

With the second car, return to Sunset Boulevard, turn left, and drive 3.7 miles east to Mandeville Canyon Road. Turn left onto Mandeville Canyon Road. At the first stop sign, turn left onto Westridge Road. Continue until you reach Cordelia Road; turn right and park. Walk up to the end of Westridge Road.

THE RUN

The trailhead (25A) is located behind the gate at the end of Westridge Road. Proceed uphill on the trail for 3.7 miles to a ranger station and an old Nike missile installation and observation tower (25B). There are picnic tables, restrooms, and water here. Enjoy sweeping views of Los Angeles from this vantage point and from the nearby observation tower. Continue north and downhill for 50 yards to the intersection of unpaved Mulholland Drive. Turn left (west) onto Mulholland Drive. At mile 4.5 pass the Sullivan Ridge Fire Road (25C) marked by the yellow metal gate. Continue west on Mulholland.

At mile 4.8 just before Mulholland begins to veer to the right, look to the left for the entrance to Topanga State Park. Head for the gated fire road on the left and follow the Farmer Ridge Trail leading southwest along the ridge (25D). Several forks in the trail over the next 0.6 mile can be a little tricky. Make a left turn at each fork. The first fork is on the ridge and parallels the main trail. The second fork leads south downhill just before the ridge ends. Immediately turn left at the third fork to avoid the steep trail leading directly downhill.

This begins a series of short switchbacks that end at a lower section of the trail avoided at the third fork. Turn left at this intersection and then make

Bent Arrow Trail

an immediate right on the narrow trail leading down to the west (25E). Follow this trail as it traces the contour of the hillside to an intersection with Mulholland Drive (25F). Turn left onto Mulholland Drive and in 0.25 mile take another left onto the Bent Arrow Trail (25G), which is marked with several signs. Take this 0.4-mile trail as it winds around a hill and then climbs a series of steep switchbacks to Fire Road No. 30 (25H). Turn left on Fire Road No. 30 and follow it uphill to the convergence of four fire roads at Hub Junction (25I). This is a great location to meet other hikers, cyclists, or runners passing by or stopping to rest.

From Hub Junction, stay to the left from the direction you arrived and continue south on the Temescal Ridge Trail. At 0.5 mile from Hub Junction you will pass the Rogers Road Trail on the left (25J). Continue straight on the Temescal Ridge Trail. At 1.8 miles from Hub Junction, Trailer Canyon Trail (25K) intersects from the right. Continue to the left up a little hill on the Temescal Ridge Trail. At mile 11.1, the Palisades Highlands Trail intersects from the right (25L). Continue straight ahead.

The trail forks at mile 11.75 (25M). Take the fork to the left. Just past this, the Waterfall Trail intersects from the left (25N). Continue to the right. From here, take the trail to the left that leads down the canyon.

At mile 12.1, Bienveneda Trail intersects from the right (25O). Continue to the left. At mile 12.6, the Leacock Trail intersects from the right (25P). Continue to the left. At mile 12.75 at a high point, take the trail to the left (25Q). At mile 13.2, a narrow trail leads off to the right toward nearby houses (25R). Avoid that trail and turn left downhill. At mile 13.3 there is a four-way intersection of small trails. Take the trail to the right heading southwest (25S). Cross a bridge at the trail's end and continue due east 100 feet to the paved walkway. Turn right on this walkway past the restroom to the parking lot.

Special Note: Approximately the first 2,000 feet of this course is across private property.

SIGNIFICANT TRAIL LANDMARKS
25A. Trailhead behind gate.
25B. Ranger station with water and toilets.
25C. Intersection of Sullivan Canyon Fire Road from the left.
25D. Entrance to Topanga State Park. Go left through gate onto Farmer Ridge Trail.
25E. Turn left at the intersection and make an immediate right on the narrow trail leading west.
25F. Intersection with Mulholland Drive. Turn left onto road.
25G. Signs mark Bent Arrow Trail. Turn left onto trail.
25H. Go left uphill on Fire Road No. 30.
25I. Hub Junction. Stay to the left from the direction you arrived and continue on the Temescal Ridge Trail.
25J. Rogers Road Trail intersects from the left. Continue straight.
25K. Trailer Canyon Road intersects from the right. Continue left.
25L. Palisades Highlands Trail intersects from the right. Continue straight ahead.

25M. Fork in the trail. Go left.

25N. Waterfall Trail intersects from the left. Continue right. From here, take the trail to the left that leads down the canyon.

25O. Bienveneda intersects from the right. Continue to the left.

25P. Leacock Trail intersects from the right. Continue to the left.

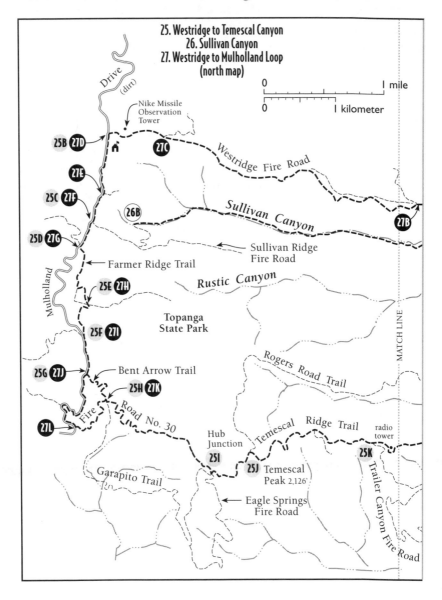

25. Westridge to Temescal Canyon
26. Sullivan Canyon
27. Westridge to Mulholland Loop
(north map)

25Q. High point. Continue to the left.

25R. Narrow trail leading right toward houses. Turn left.

25S. Four-way intersection. Turn right (southwest) toward the finish. Follow the paved walkway to restrooms, the parking lot, and Sunset Boulevard.

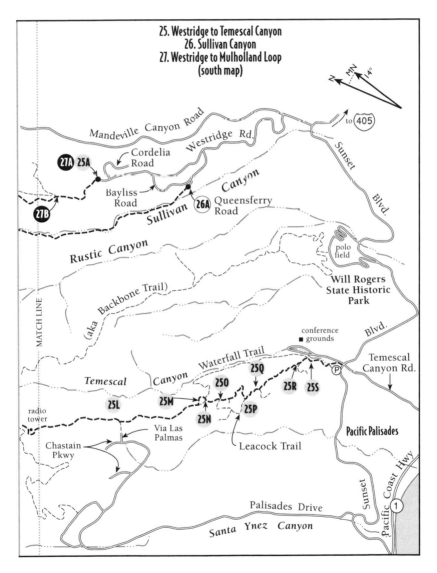

26
Sullivan Canyon

Distance: 8.2 miles
Course geometry: Out and back
Running time: 1.25–2 hours
Start altitude: 700 feet
Finish altitude: 700 feet
Elevation gain: 920 feet
Highest altitude: 1,550 feet
Difficulty: Moderate
Water: None
Area management: Topanga State Park
Maps: Topanga (USGS)
    Trail Map of the Santa Monica Mountains, East

This course through scenic Sullivan Canyon has many exciting stream cross-ings beneath heavy foliage. The stream crossings are straightforward during the summer. After a rain, however, water levels rise, providing opportunities to get your feet wet. Run under a delightful, rich green canopy of tall trees and enjoy the peaceful atmosphere.

GETTING THERE

From the San Diego Freeway (Interstate 405), take Sunset Boulevard and continue west 2.3 miles to Mandeville Canyon. Turn right and continue to

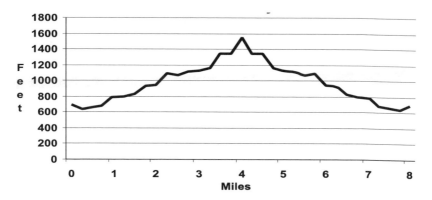

Foliage in Sullivan Canyon

the first stop sign. Turn left. Proceed up Westridge Road and turn left on Bayliss Road. Continue to Queensferry Road. The trail begins at the end of Queensferry Road, but parking is restricted, so park up the street in an unrestricted zone.

THE RUN

Go down Queensferry Road (26A) past the large gate at the end of the pavement and turn right at the bottom of Sullivan Canyon. The trail follows the canyon floor and crosses the stream several times. Several smaller trails branch off from the main trail along the way, but they eventually return to the main trail. The canyon is relatively flat and is a popular biking route, so watch closely for cyclists.

You will enjoy this easy run through the canyon. At mile 3.9 just after crossing a 30-inch-wide concrete drainage culvert, the trail turns sharply to the left and ascends steeply into the chaparral (26B). This marks the turnaround point. Return to the start on the same course.

SIGNIFICANT TRAIL LANDMARKS

26A. Trailhead behind gate at end of pavement. Turn right at bottom of canyon.

26B. Concrete culvert at mile 3.9. Return to the start the way you came.

27
Westridge to Mulholland Loop

Distance: 14 miles
Course geometry: Out-and-back loop
Running time: 2–3.5 hours
Start altitude: 1,260 feet
Finish altitude: 1,260 feet
Elevation gain: 1,900 feet
Highest altitude: 1,960 feet
Difficulty: Moderate
Water: At the ranger station
Area management: California Department of Parks and Recreation
    Santa Monica Mountains Conservancy
    Mountains Recreation and Conservation Authority
Maps: Topanga and Canoga Park (USGS)
    Trail Map of the Santa Monica Mountains, East

Enjoy a moderate 3.7-mile climb to a crest of the Santa Monica Mountains with views of the Los Angeles Basin and the San Fernando Valley. At the historic Nike missile site, stop and climb up to the observation deck for incredible views in all directions. As you run down Mulholland Drive, there are spectacular views of the San Fernando Valley.

GETTING THERE

From the San Diego Freeway (Interstate 405), take Sunset Boulevard west 2.3 miles to Mandeville Canyon; turn right and continue to the first stop sign. Turn left on Westridge Road and drive until you reach Cordelia Road. Turn right and park. Walk up to the end of Westridge Road.

THE RUN

The trailhead (27A) is behind the gate where the pavement ends on Westridge Road. Proceed uphill on the dirt road for 3.7 miles, avoiding the trails at 0.5 mile (27B) and 3.1 miles (27C) that intersect from the right. The ranger station located at the old Nike missile installation and observation tower (27D) has picnic tables, restrooms, and water. Enjoy sweeping views

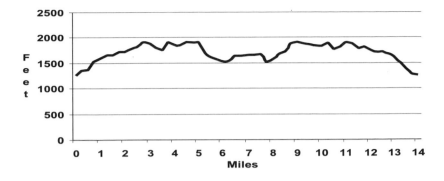

of Los Angeles from this vantage point and from the nearby observation tower. Continue north and downhill for 50 yards to the intersection with unpaved Mulholland Drive. Turn left and head west on Mulholland Drive, passing a trail intersecting on the left (27E). At mile 4.3, just after running under large lines, pass the Sullivan Ridge Fire Road (27F) behind a yellow metal gate.

Continue on Mulholland Drive and at mile 4.8 just before Mulholland Drive begins to veer to the right, look to the left for the entrance to Topanga State Park. Head for the gated fire road on the left and follow the Farmer Ridge Trail (27G) southwest along the ridge.

Several forks in the trail over the next 0.6 mile can be a little tricky. Make a left turn at each fork. The first fork is on the ridge and parallels the main trail. The second fork leads south downhill just before the ridge ends. Immediately turn left on the third fork to avoid the steep trail leading directly downhill. This begins a series of short switchbacks that end at the lower section of trail avoided at the third fork. Turn left at this intersection and then make an immediate right on the narrow trail leading down to the west (27H). Follow this trail as it traces the contour of the hillside to an intersection with Mulholland Drive (27I).

Turn left onto Mulholland Drive and in 0.25 mile take another left onto the Bent Arrow Trail, which is marked with several signs (27J). Take this 0.4-mile trail as it winds around a hill and then climbs a series of steep switchbacks to Fire Road No. 30 (27K). Turn right on Fire Road No. 30 and follow it uphill to where it intersects with Mulholland Drive (27L). Turn right and run north around a hill and then east down a steep hill. At the bottom of the hill is the intersection with the Bent Arrow Trail (27J) on the right. Return to the start the way you came.

Special Note: Approximately the first 2,000 feet of this course is across private property.

Lizard along trail

SIGNIFICANT TRAIL LANDMARKS

27A. Trailhead behind gate.

27B. Trail intersects from the right. Stay left.

27C. Trail intersects from the right. Stay left.

27D. Ranger station.

27E. Continue past the restrooms to Mulholland Drive. Turn left onto unpaved road.

27F. Sullivan Canyon Fire Road intersects on the left behind gate. Continue on Mulholland Drive.

27G. Entrance to Topanga State Park. Turn left onto Farmer Ridge Trail behind gate.

27H. Turn left at the intersection and then make an immediate right onto the narrow trail.

27I. Intersection with Mulholland Drive. Turn left onto road.

27J. Signs mark Bent Arrow Trail, turn left onto trail.

27K. Intersection with Fire Road No. 30. Turn right uphill onto fire road.

27L. Intersection with Mulholland Drive. Turn right onto road. Continue to intersection with Bent Arrow Trail (27J); then return to the start the way you came.

28
Catalina/Avalon Loop

Distance: 8.6 miles
Course geometry: Loop
Running time: 1.5–2.5 hours
Start altitude: 730 feet
Finish altitude: 10 feet
Highest altitude: 1,510 feet
Elevation gain: 900 feet
Difficulty: Moderate
Water: At the start and finish
Area management: Catalina Island Conservancy
Maps: Santa Catalina (USGS)

What could be nicer than to visit a romantic city on a fascinating island? The course is a gem and starts within walking distance from the harbor and hotels. The trailhead is inside the Wrigley Memorial and Botanical Gardens where you can view an extensive collection of plants and cactus native to the Channel Islands.

The course is on a wide, smooth dirt road, with delightful views of Avalon and the Los Angeles Basin across the channel. The trails have unobtrusive markers with distance and trail initials. The narrow ridgeline features unobstructed views of San Clemente Island and the rugged west side of Catalina. California holly and lemonade berry are abundant, wonderful cactus bloom on the sunnier ridges all summer, and eucalyptus trees line the downhill

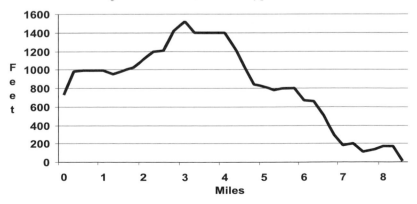

return. The course finishes at the beach, where you can take a refreshing dip to cool off. The city is fun to explore and a tour of the historic casino building is highly recommended.

Before the run, make sure that your shoes are free of dirt that may have any type of seeds attached. This helps prevent the introduction of non-native plants to this delicate ecosystem. All plants and wildlife are protected and should not be disturbed. Please do not chase the buffalo or other wildlife because they will become skittish and other visitors will not be able to enjoy them.

Catalina is a private island preserved by the Catalina Island Conservancy. It is open to the public, but a free permit is required to hike or run on the trails. Obtain the permit after you reach the island.

GETTING THERE

From San Pedro or Long Beach, take a ferry to Avalon. Helicopter service is also available. To obtain a permit to use the trails, walk one block from the beach to visitor services at the Catalina Island Conservancy, 125 Claressa

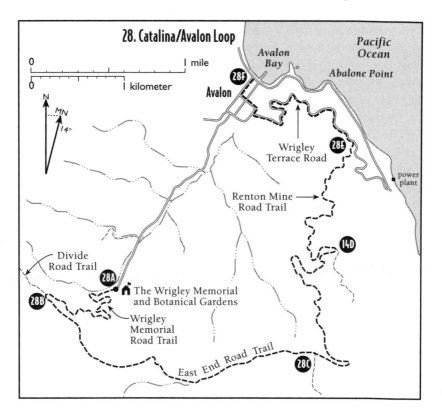

Avalon Harbor at Catalina Island

Avenue; telephone 310-510-2595. The conservancy is open from 9 A.M. to 5 P.M., 7 days a week. Coin lockers are available nearby to store your gear if desired.

Walk or jog 1.5 miles along the paved Avalon Canyon Road past the golf course and horse stables until it dead-ends at the Wrigley Memorial and Botanical Gardens. The trailhead is inside the gate. There is a $3 fee to enter. There is no water on the course after you leave the botanical garden area, so carry plenty with you.

THE RUN

After exploring the botanical garden (28A), proceed uphill on the wide dirt road to Wrigley Memorial just ahead. The start of Wrigley Memorial Road Trail is through a gate to the right of the memorial. Enjoy wonderful views of Avalon as you climb the 1.2 miles to the ridge. The vegetation is lush in the canyon, and prickly pear cactus grows on the sunnier ridges. When the trail meets the East End Road Trail and the Divide Road Trail at the ridge (28B), go left onto the East End Road Trail. The view of San Clemente Island and the west side of Catalina is breathtaking.

Continue for 2.6 miles to a fork in the dirt road (28C), and turn left onto the upper road. After 1.6 miles you will come to an intersection (28D) with the Renton Mine Road Trail. Turn left. Eucalyptus trees line this dirt road, providing welcome shade. In 1.4 miles the dirt road ends at the paved Upper Terrace Road (28E); go left. After a 300-yard hill, you will see one of the most beautiful vistas of Avalon imaginable. Continue down the road until you get to the pier, the finish of this run. The cool water at the beach is quite refreshing, so jump in.

SIGNIFICANT TRAIL LANDMARKS

28A. Trailhead inside Wrigley Memorial and Botanical Gardens. Wrigley Memorial Road Trail is through a gate to the right of the memorial.

28B. Intersection with East End Road Trail and Divide Road Trail. Go left onto East End Road Trail.

28C. Fork in the road. Turn left onto upper road.

28D. Intersection with the Renton Mine Road Trail. Turn left.

28E. The dirt road ends at Wrigley Terrace Road. Go left 300 yards over a hill. Avalon is in sight.

28F. Finish at the pier.

29

Franklin Canyon Loop

Distance: 5.5 miles

Course geometry: Loop

Running time: 0.75–1.5 hours

Start altitude: 830 feet

Finish altitude: 830 feet

Elevation gain: 1,400 feet

Highest altitude: 1,100 feet

Difficulty: Easy

Water: At the start and at point 29G

Area management: Santa Monica Mountains Conservancy
   Mountains Recreation and Conservation Authority
   National Park Service

Maps: Beverly Hills (USGS)

Franklin Canyon is a wonderful treasure between Hollywood and Beverly Hills. This island of open space has lush trails with forests of eucalyptus, oak, and sycamore trees. There are ponds with ducks, small streams, wildflowers galore, and city views. There are restrooms, telephones, and water at the beginning and at the turnaround point. This run has it all—you will not believe you are in the middle of the city.

GETTING THERE

From the Ventura Freeway (Interstate 101), go south on Coldwater Canyon Drive 2.5 miles and then turn right (west) on Franklin Canyon Drive.

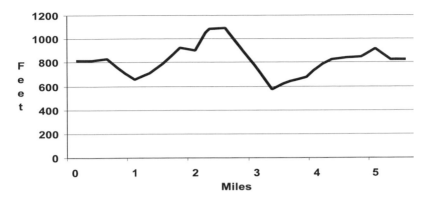

Continue 0.5 mile to the William O. Douglas Outdoor Classroom (a botanical garden); park in the parking lot on the left. From Sunset Boulevard, go north on North Beverly Drive. This becomes Coldwater Canyon Avenue and then joins Mulholland Drive northbound. Go left as Coldwater joins Mulholland, and at the intersection with Coldwater Canyon and Franklin Canyon Drive turn left. Continue 0.5 mile to the William O. Douglas Outdoor Classroom; park in the parking lot on the left. Parking is free.

THE RUN

From the parking lot (29A), run south on the paved road staying to the right of the white buildings. You will pass Heavenly Pond on the right and then cross a scenic bridge with Franklin Canyon Lake on the left. Watch for the serene ducks floating quietly on the lake.

Where the road ends at a paved intersection, continue straight ahead onto the single-track trail just to the right of the stop sign (29B). This trail is lined with poison oak, so make your way downhill carefully. After crossing a bridge (29C), turn left on paved Lake Drive. A stream follows the road. Continue for 0.5 mile and then turn left through a yellow gate alongside a gravel parking area onto the Hastain Trail (29D) leading uphill.

In less than a mile the fire road makes a sharp bend to the left. A small single-track trail to the right is the return trail (29E) that you will take on the way back. A "NO BIKES" sign marks the entrance to this smaller trail. From here, you can look down at the Franklin Canyon Reservoir and Century City. Continue up the fire road for another 0.5 mile to the top (29F).

After enjoying the views, return down the hill back to point E. Take the single-track trail downhill, enter a grassy park (29G), cross the park in a northerly direction, and proceed uphill on the paved road. The park has picnic tables, restrooms, water, and a pay phone. A smaller trail parallels the paved

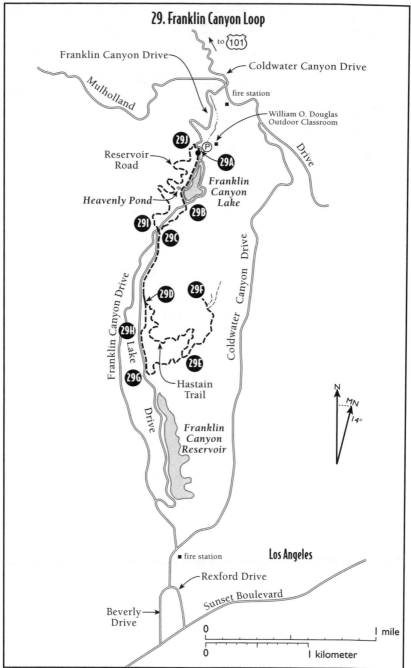

29. Franklin Canyon Loop

to 101

Franklin Canyon Drive

Coldwater Canyon Drive

Mulholland

fire station

William O. Douglas
Outdoor Classroom

Drive

29J

P

Reservoir
Road

29A

*Franklin
Canyon
Lake*

Heavenly Pond

29B

29I

29C

Franklin Canyon Drive

29D

29F

Lake

29H

Coldwater Canyon Drive

29E

29G

Hastain
Trail

Drive

*Franklin
Canyon
Reservoir*

N
MN
14°

fire station **Los Angeles**

Rexford Drive

Sunset Boulevard

Beverly
Drive

0   1 mile

0   1 kilometer

Blooming yucca

ιυad on the right (29H) for 0.25 mile before rejoining the paved road.

After another mile, you will see the old paved Reservoir Road on the left, which has concrete barriers and a "CLOSED TO VEHICLES" sign (29I). Take this scenic road north. It begins paved, but becomes a dirt road before rejoining paved Franklin Canyon Road (29J). This is where you turn right downhill for 0.25 mile back to the parking lot. The nature center located at the parking area is worth exploring.

SIGNIFICANT TRAIL LANDMARKS

29A. Run south on paved road staying to the right of white buildings.

29B. Paved intersection. Go straight on single-track trail to the right of stop sign.

29C. Bridge crossing. Turn left onto Lake Drive.

29D. Yellow gate next to parking area. Turn left through gate onto Hastain Trail.

29E. Small trail to right marked with a "NO BIKES" sign. This trail will be taken on the return.

29F. Summit of the fire road. Return downhill and take the small trail at Landmark E.

29G. Grassy park. Cross in a northerly direction to the paved road.

29H. Optional trail to the right parallels the road for 0.25 mile.

29I. Reservoir Road on the left with concrete barriers and "CLOSED TO VEHICLES" sign. Take road to the north.

29J. Franklin Canyon Drive. Go to the right downhill to the parking lot.

30
Griffith Park to Mount Hollywood

Distance: 5.25 miles
Course geometry: Out-and-back
Running time: 0.7–1.5 hours
Start altitude: 630 feet
Finish altitude: 630 feet
Elevation gain: 1,200 feet
Highest altitude: 1,625 feet
Difficulty: Easy
Water: Several locations
Area management: Griffith Park
Maps: Burbank and Los Angeles (USGS)

This delightful course is ideal for newcomers to trail running in Los Angeles. The wide, smooth fire roads are popular with walkers, runners, and equestrians. There are several water stops and rest areas under shady trees. Those who do not want to go the entire distance can explore the Griffith Park Observatory before returning to the start. The landscape is scenic, the city views superb, and you will catch glimpses of the Hollywood sign on the mountain to the west. Parking is free.

GETTING THERE

From the Santa Monica Freeway (Interstate 10), take the Western Avenue exit and drive north 5 miles to its end, turn right, and make an immediate

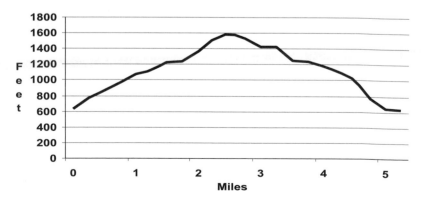

left turn onto Fern Dell Drive. Continue 0.3 mile to the parking area. The parking area closes at sunset.

THE RUN

Head past the restrooms and through an area of ponds to reach the trailhead (30A). Follow the stream uphill on either one of two fire roads (30B) to Griffith Observatory. The two fire roads join in about 0.25 mile (30C). You can see the Hollywood sign on the mountain to your left. Enjoy wonderful views of the Los Angeles Basin and the downtown area from the knoll 300 feet below the observatory (30D).

Go up to the observatory and continue north through the parking lot to the Charlie Turner Trail (30E). Follow this well-maintained trail to a bridge crossing. Continue to follow the wide fire road to where it joins another fire road (30F). Go left and continue to Mount Hollywood peak (30G).

After enjoying the splendid views, return downhill and go to the right on the fire road. When you return to the intersection of the fire roads (30F), go left downhill the way you came. Remember that when you cross the bridge you need to go left up the short hill to return the way you came.

Hollywood sign

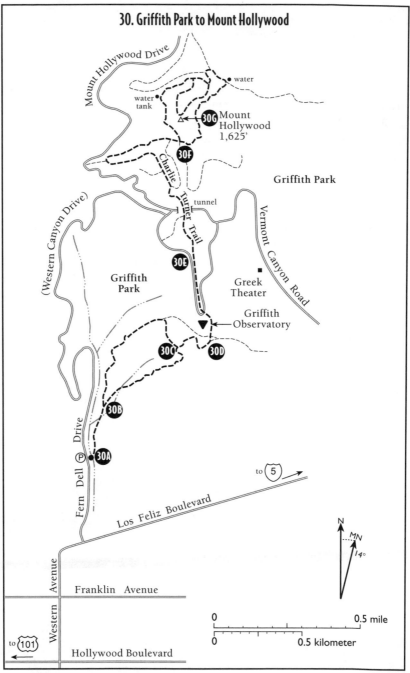

30. Griffith Park to Mount Hollywood

SIGNIFICANT TRAIL LANDMARKS

30A. Trailhead is past restrooms near ponds.

30B. Two fire roads lead to observatory. Take either one.

30C. Convergence of the two fire roads.

30D. Knoll 300 feet below observatory.

30E. Pick up Charlie Turner Trail at north end of parking area.

30F. Intersection with fire road. Go left to Mount Hollywood peak.

30G. Mount Hollywood peak. Return downhill and go right on the fire road.

31
Cheeseboro Canyon

Distance: 12.5 miles

Course geometry: Out-and-back loop

Running time: 1.75–3.5 hours

Start altitude: 1,050 feet

Finish altitude: 1,050 feet

Elevation gain: 1,200 feet

Highest altitude: 2,075 feet

Difficulty: Moderate

Water: None

Area management: Santa Monica Mountain National Park Recreation
    Area

Maps: Calabasas (USGS)
    Santa Monica Mountains, Trails Illustrated

This delightful trail begins along an old ranch road and crosses a shallow streambed nestled in an oak-filled canyon. After 4 miles, the trail narrows and winds along chaparral slopes with wonderful vistas of valleys and mountains. An abundance of wildflowers borders the trails in the spring. Deer and coyotes can be seen year-round.

GETTING THERE

From the Ventura Freeway (Interstate 101), take the Chesebro Road exit. Turn right on Palo Comado Canyon Road and turn right on Chesebro Road. Proceed 0.7 mile and turn right into the public parking lot. If the gate is locked, park on the side of the road and walk to the trailhead at the parking area.

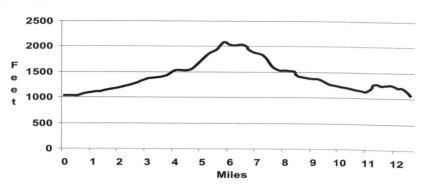

THE RUN

A wooden turnstile at the north end of the parking lot marks the beginning of the Cheeseboro Canyon Trail, which heads east (31A). At 0.6 mile, Canyon View Trail intersects from the right (31B). Continue straight ahead.

In 1.3 miles you will come to a four-way intersection with the Baleen Wall Trail on the right and the Palo Comado Connector on the left (31C). Go straight ahead on Sulphur Springs Trail. The trail forks at 1.6 miles (31D); continue straight ahead to the junction of the Ranch Center Trail (31E). At mile 3.3, cross the sulphur springs, easily recognizable by the pungent odor and white opaque hue to the water (31F). The trail narrows at this point.

Continue to the Shephards Flat intersection at mile 4 (31G). Take the left trail going west. After 200 feet, the trail forks. Take the right fork; these two short trails rejoin in 400 feet (31H). As you climb out of the valley (31I), take a sharp left up to the rise. Avoid the narrow, barely perceptible trails leading off to the right that are fenced off.

Coming around a rise, you will see a magnificent view of the valley below (31J). At mile 5, the trail joins with the wide Palo Comado Canyon Trail (31K).

Continue uphill to the right. At 6.1 miles, there is an old sheep corral on the right with wooden fences and old farm equipment (31L). This is the turnaround point, but if you wish to add mileage in this pretty countryside, simply continue on the fire road as far as you wish and return to the start the way you came. On the return, remember you came in on the trail off the fire road and to the left at mile 7.2 (1.1 miles from the sheep corral). It is easy to miss on the way back.

About 100 yards beyond the lookout point (31J), at the fork at mile 7.5, take the trail to the left. The trail follows the rise to the left and then the fork that goes sharply downhill into the valley (31I). Continue right at the next intersection (31H) and right again at Shepherds Flat (31G), mile 8.2. Return to the start the way you came.

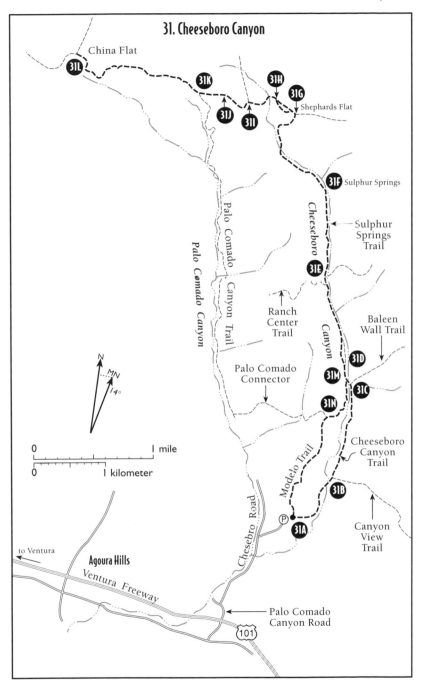

31. Cheeseboro Canyon

China Flat

31L

31K

31H

31G

Shephards Flat

31J **31I**

31F Sulphur Springs

Cheeseboro

Sulphur
Springs
Trail

Palo Comado Canyon Trail

Palo Comado Canyon

31E

Ranch
Center
Trail

Canyon

Baleen
Wall Trail

Palo Comado
Connector

31D

31M

31C

N
MN
14°

31N

Cheeseboro
Canyon
Trail

0   1 mile

0   1 kilometer

Modelo Trail

31B

P

31A

Canyon
View
Trail

Chesebro Road

to Ventura

Agoura Hills

Ventura Freeway

Palo Comado
Canyon Road

101

Cheeseboro Canyon

Option: A challenging alternative on the return route is to take the Palo Comado Connector (31M) to the right at mile 10.8. At the top of a steep hill, sweeping views of the surrounding area make the tough, short climb worth the effort. The Palo Comado Connector joins the Modelo Trail on the left at mile 11.3 (31N). Take the Modelo Trail the last 1.2 miles down to the parking area.

SIGNIFICANT TRAIL LANDMARKS

31A. Cheeseboro Canyon Trailhead at north end of parking lot through turnstile.

31B. Intersection with Canyon View Trail. Continue straight ahead.

31C. Four-way intersection. Go straight ahead on Sulphur Springs Trail.

31D. Fork in the trail. Continue straight ahead.

31E. Junction with Ranch Center Trail. Continue straight ahead.

31F. Sulphur spring crossing.

31G. Intersection with Shepards Flat. Go left and then take a right at the fork.

31H. Continue straight ahead when the two trails converge.

31I. Take a sharp left up to the rise.

31J. Lookout point on the left.

31K. Intersection with the Palo Comado Canyon Trail. Take note of this area so you do not miss it on the way back.

31L. Turnaround point at sheep corral. Return the way you came or take the optional route (31M).

31M. Intersection with Palo Comado Connector to the right.

31N. Intersection with the Modelo Trail. Follow Modelo Trail to the parking area.

32
Old Stagecoach Road

Distance: 4 miles
Course geometry: Out and back
Running time: 0.75–1.25 hours
Start altitude: 1,000 feet
Finish altitude: 1,000 feet
Elevation gain: 1,050 feet
Highest altitude: 1,800 feet
Difficulty: Easy
Water: At the start and finish
Area management: California Department of Parks and Recreation
   Rancho Simi Recreation and Park District
Maps: Simi Valley East and Oat Mountain (USGS)

The Simi Hills are a vital wildlife corridor between several mountain ranges.
This unique area features beautiful sandstone rock formations. Stagecoaches
traveled through these rocky hills on the Old Stagecoach Road. Running
here brings to mind the many classic movie Westerns filmed nearby.

GETTING THERE
   Take either Ventura Freeway (Interstate 101) or the Ronald Reagan Freeway
(State Highway 118) to the Topanga Canyon Boulevard exit. From the Ventura
Freeway, drive north on Topanga Canyon Boulevard to Devonshire Street and
turn left. From the Ronald Reagan Freeway, drive south on Topanga Canyon

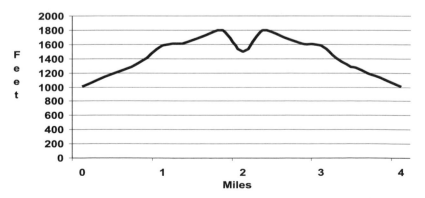

Boulevard to Devonshire Street and turn right. Devonshire ends in 1 mile at a driveway leading into Chatsworth Park South. Proceed up the driveway to the parking lot. The trailhead is at the far west end of the park. Parking is free. The park closes at sunset.

THE RUN

The trailhead is on the west side of Chatsworth Park South (32A). Follow the trail up a rocky hill amid huge sandstone boulders common in this area. At the top of the short hill, turn right on the asphalt road and descend. At the bottom of the hill, take the trail to the left (32B). At the top of the next hill, take the trail to the right leading west along a row of olive trees on the left (32C). This trail ends at the intersection of a north-south trail; turn right here (32D). Watch carefully for a trail leading away to the left as you round the mountain (32E). Turn left at this trail and begin climbing up the slope toward the pass. Look for the white tile marker halfway up identifying the Old Stagecoach Road.

Progress may slow as the trail proceeds over sandstone rock with many large steps. In rainy weather, this section of trail becomes a small stream, but this should not cause difficulty. This is the steepest section of the run and it is

difficult to imagine stagecoaches making their way through here.

At the top of the hill, the rocks give way to a dirt trail and level ground (32F). Follow the main trail straight ahead to a chain-link fence (32G). A trail on the right leads north to an opening in the fence where there is a bulletin board. Go through the fence and follow the trail to the right.

The trail winds around several short hills and shallow canyons. Views of Simi Valley open as you approach Santa Susana Pass Road and State Highway 118 to the north.

Old Stagecoach Road
(Photo by Jim Wolff)

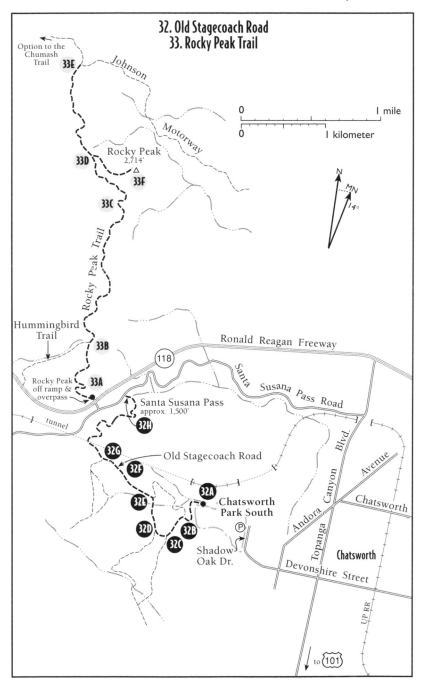

32. Old Stagecoach Road
33. Rocky Peak Trail

Option to the Chumash Trail

33E

Johnson

Motorway

Rocky Peak
2,714'
△

33D

33F

33C

0   I mile

0   I kilometer

N
MN
14°

Rocky Peak Trail

Hummingbird Trail

33B

Ronald Reagan Freeway

118

Santa Susana Pass Road

Rocky Peak off ramp & overpass

33A

tunnel

Santa Susana Pass
approx. 1,500'

32H

32G

Old Stagecoach Road

32F

32A

32E

Chatsworth
Park South

32D

32B

32C

Shadow
Oak Dr.

P

Topanga Canyon Blvd.

Andora Avenue

Chatsworth

Chatsworth

Devonshire Street

UP RR

to 101

The trail ends with a descent to Santa Susana Pass Road (32H) just east of the Rocky Peak overpass. Return to the start the same way you came.

Option: If you want to cover more distance, continue on the Rocky Peak Trail directly across the Rocky Peak overpass (refer to Run No. 33, Rocky Peak Trail).

SIGNIFICANT TRAIL LANDMARKS

32A. Trailhead on the west side of park.

32B. Turn right at intersection with paved road. At bottom of hill, turn left onto trail.

32C. At top of hill, turn right and follow the olive trees.

32D. Trail ends at intersection. Turn right.

32E. Round mountain and watch for trail on left. Turn left.

32F. Rocky section gives way to level ground.

32G. Chain-link fence. Go through fence and take trail to the right.

32H. Santa Susana Pass Road. Return to the start the same way you came.

33
Rocky Peak Trail

Distance: 7 miles

Course geometry: Out and back

Running time: 1.25–2.5 hours

Start altitude: 1,575 feet

Finish altitude: 1,575 feet

Elevation gain: 1,200 feet

Highest altitude: 2,714 feet

Difficulty: Moderate

Water: None

Area management: Santa Monica Mountain Conservancy
 Mountains Recreation and Conservation Authority
 Rancho Simi Recreation and Park District
 City of Simi Valley

Maps: Simi Valley East (USGS)

The Rocky Peak Trail is in the picturesque Simi Hills, known for wonderful sandstone formations. This wide fire road is popular with cyclists and hikers and has excellent views of the San Fernando and Simi Valleys. Runners will

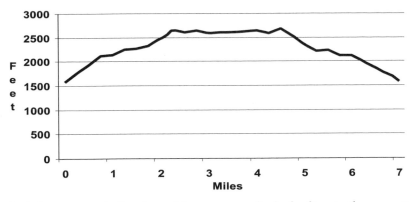

find this course challenging with two steep climbs leading to the summit ridge. Connections to several other trails create excellent opportunities for longer courses.

GETTING THERE

Take the Ronald Reagan Freeway (State Highway 118) and exit at the Rocky Peak off ramp at the summit of the Santa Susana Pass 2 miles west of Topanga Canyon Boulevard. From Simi Valley, take the Santa Susana Pass Road east to the Rocky Peak overpass. When traveling east, there is no off ramp from the Ronald Reagan Freeway at Rocky Peak. The trailhead is located at the north end of the Rocky Peak overpass. Free parking is available near the trailhead or on Santa Susana Pass Road.

THE RUN

Starting from behind a large green metal gate and a bulletin board with information about the area (33A), the Rocky Peak Trail begins with a steep 50-yard section. After a series of switchbacks during the first 0.6 mile, you will pass the Hummingbird Trail (33B) on the left marked with a large post and a bench. Do not take this trail. Stay on the Rocky Peak Trail, which passes by large sandstone formations surrounded by grasses, sage, and laurel sumac. This is a dry and windy area and consequently has few trees.

After 1.5 miles, the trail levels as it enters a wide valley along the ridge. Rocky Peak summit is visible to the north. Notice the Rocky Peak Trail below the summit ridge as it climbs steeply 0.5 mile toward the ridge. A large oak tree (33C) located at 1.9 miles will provide welcome shade on a hot day. Just after cresting the Rocky Peak ridge at 2.3 miles, you will pass a narrow trail heading off to the right that leads to Rocky Peak (33D). Continue on the main Rocky Peak Trail.

Rocky Peak Trail (Photo by Jim Wolff)

Spectacular views of the Santa Monica Mountains, from Mugu Peak to Hollywood, Simi Valley, and beyond to the distant Santa Ynez Mountains above Santa Barbara, are now in view. To the north, the slopes of Oat Mountain in the Santa Susana Range join with the Simi Hills in green rolling valleys and canyons.

For the next 0.7 mile, the trail rolls over gentle hills to the intersection with the Johnson Motorway (33E). Despite the name, there are no cars on Johnson Motorway. This narrow trail marked with a small wood post leads east down into the San Fernando Valley ending near Topanga Canyon. Turn around at the intersection and return to the start the same way you came.

Option 1: From the intersection with Johnson Motorway, continue north on the Rocky Peak Trail for 1 mile to the junction with the Chumash Trail. The Chumash Trail leads west 2.4 miles down into Simi Valley eventually terminating in Chumash Park located at the end of Flanagan Road. Turn around whenever you're ready and return the way you came.

Option 2: If time permits, take the narrow trail (33D) leading to the Rocky Peak summit (33F). The trail ends on a small peak about 0.25 mile short of the actual summit. The faint trail heads west to another slightly higher peak. Scramble down a narrow canyon and then up 100 feet to the Rocky Peak summit. Magnificent views reward your effort to reach this point. It can be incredibly windy here, however. Return to the start on the same course.

SIGNIFICANT TRAIL LANDMARKS

33A. Trail starts behind metal gate.

33B. Pass the Hummingbird Trail on the left.

33C. Large oak tree.

33D. Trail to the summit of Rocky Peak on the right at mile 2.3.

33E. Intersection with Johnson Motorway. Look for a small wood post.

33F. Rocky Peak summit.

SAN GABRIEL MOUNTAINS
Los Angeles, Pasadena, Claremont, Rancho Cucamonga

The San Gabriel Mountains dominate the northern border of the Los Angeles Basin. They rise dramatically to 10,064 feet at the summit of Mount San Antonio (Mount Baldy), the third highest mountain in Southern California. This wonderful range separates Los Angeles from the great Mojave Desert.

In addition to sage scrub and chaparral, sycamore- and oak-filled canyons are at the lower elevations with fragrant pine forests higher up. The fantastic views of Los Angeles, the mountain range, and the Mojave Desert are incredible.

An extensive network of trails makes this area a perfect location for moderate- to high-altitude running. Take it slow at first to avoid getting short of breath until you get used to running at higher altitudes. Bring plenty of water and always carry a map and a compass. Most of the trails are well marked and easy to follow, but it is best to be prepared.

An Adventure Pass is required to park in Angeles, San Bernardino, Los

Padres, and Cleveland National Forests. You can purchase an Adventure Pass for $5 per day or $30 per year at ranger stations and sporting goods stores.

Placerita Canyon

Distance: 8.5 miles
Course geometry: Out and back
Running time: 1.1–2.2 hours
Start altitude: 1,525 feet
Finish altitude: 1,525 feet
Elevation gain: 1,640 feet
Highest altitude: 3,166 feet
Difficulty: Moderate
Water: At the start and midway (34B)
Area management: Placerita Canyon Natural Area
   Los Angeles County Parks and Recreation
Maps: Mint Canyon and San Fernando (USGS)
   Trails of Angeles Front Country

This wonderful area in Santa Clarita features a gentle creek with lush shrubbery, grasses, colorful flowers, and sycamore trees. You can shorten the run and turn around at Walker Ranch 2 miles from the trailhead after exploring the waterfall, or enjoy an invigorating run up Los Piñetos Trail to see lovely views of the Santa Clarita Valley. The area is full of birds, small lizards, squirrels, and foxes. The campground at the trailhead has nature and gold mining exhibits and a large picnic area with short hiking trails the entire family can enjoy.

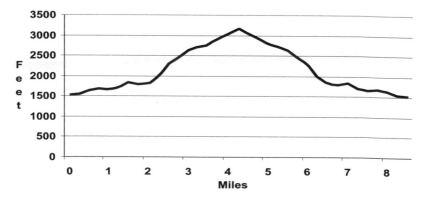

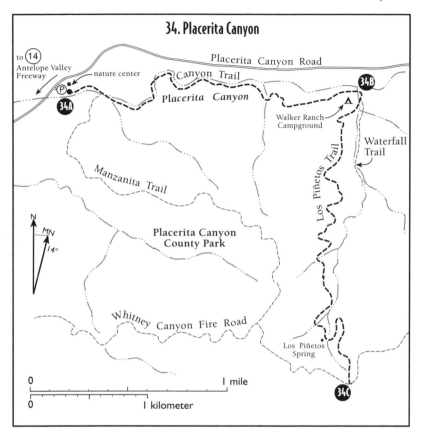

34. Placerita Canyon

GETTING THERE

Drive north on the San Diego Freeway (Interstate 405); it eventually joins the Golden State Freeway (Interstate 5). In approximately 4 miles, take the Antelope Valley Freeway (Interstate 14) 2.5 miles to Placerita Canyon Road and exit. Turn right and follow the signs 1.5 miles to the nature center parking lot on the right. Parking is $3 (an Adventure Pass is not required). The center is open 9 A.M. to 5 P.M. daily.

THE RUN

The Canyon Trail begins across from the nature center (34A) and continues for 2 miles to Walker Ranch Campground (34B). The trail is slightly rolling and has a few creek crossings. It is shaded by trees, shrubs, and steep canyon walls. The campground has portable toilets, water, and picnic benches in an oak glen.

From Walker Ranch Campground go right on Los Piñetos Trail. This scenic trail is moderately steep, but entirely runnable. The vegetation varies from yuccas and wildflowers to oak trees and poison oak. In 2.3 miles, the trail joins Whitney Canyon Fire Road on a ridge (34C), from which you'll have wonderful views of the San Fernando Valley and Santa Clarita. Enjoy the views and return the way you came. The nature center and other exhibits at the trailhead are well worth exploring.

Option: Take the Waterfall Trail from Walker Ranch Campground about 0.5 mile to cool grottos and a little waterfall. This requires some climbing on rock faces and around boulders.

SIGNIFICANT TRAIL LANDMARKS
34A. Canyon Trail begins across from the nature center.
34B. Walker Ranch Campground. Go right on Los Piñetos Trail.
34C. Intersection with Whitney Canyon Fire Road. This is the turnaround point.

35
Haines Canyon to Mount Lukens

Distance: 11.5 miles
Course geometry: Out and back
Running time: 1.5–3 hours
Start altitude: 2,160 feet
Finish altitude: 2,160 feet
Elevation gain: 3,100 feet
Highest altitude: 5,050 feet
Difficulty: Moderate
Water: None
Area management: Angeles National Forest
Maps: Sunland and Condor Peak (USGS)
    Trails of Angeles Front Country

This is a great course leading to the summit of Mount Lukens near the western end of the San Gabriel Mountains overlooking Sunland, Tujunga, the San Fernando Valley, and the Verdugo Mountains. At 5,078 feet, it is the

Placerita Canyon

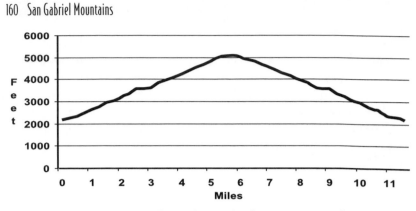

highest summit in Los Angeles and provides fantastic views of the city and surrounding mountains. It can be quite cold and windy at this altitude, so check the weather conditions in advance and plan accordingly.

GETTING THERE

Drive east on the Foothill Freeway (Interstate 210) toward Tujunga and get off at the Sunland Boulevard exit. Turn left. After passing under the freeway, this becomes Foothill Boulevard. Turn left on Apperson Street and drive to Haines Canyon Avenue and turn left. Drive to the end of Haines Canyon Avenue until it dead-ends at a gate. Park on the street.

Driving west on the Foothill Freeway toward Tujunga, get off on Honolulu Avenue and turn right. At Tujunga Canyon Boulevard, turn right. Drive to Haines Canyon Avenue and turn right. At Day Street, turn right and drive two blocks to a left turn onto Haines Canyon Avenue. Drive until the avenue dead-ends at a gate. Park on the street, taking care to avoid blocking driveways. Parking is limited. There are no restrooms or water at the trailhead or on the course.

THE RUN

The trailhead (35A) is on the right side of a gate at the end of Haines Canyon Avenue. Follow the short trail to a fire road that passes by a small dam and catch basin filled with water on the right. The fire road forks as you pass the reservoir, with the right fork leading down to the catch basin. Take the left fork (35B). Just beyond the catch basin, another fire road leads to the left. Continue straight on the fire road going into Haines Canyon, which is filled with oaks, sycamores, and a small stream. A steady climb on the fire road leads to a junction with a trail to the left and Mount Lukens Road (35C) on the right.

Mount Lukens Road is a wide fire road that follows a serpentine route to the 5,078-foot summit of Mount Lukens. This steady climb has incredible views of Los Angeles and the surrounding canyons. At the top of the fire road

(35D), turn right onto the Mount Lukens Truck Road and continue up to the summit (35E) marked by power poles and some large antennas surrounded by a chain-link fence. Return to the start the way you came.

Option: If more distance is desired, continue east on the Mount Lukens Truck Road and then return on the same course. Another option is to run west on the Mount Lukens Truck Road past Mount Lukens Road to the intersection with the Stone Canyon Trail on the right. This trail leads down into Big Tujunga Canyon and will require a second climb up to Mount Lukens to return to the start.

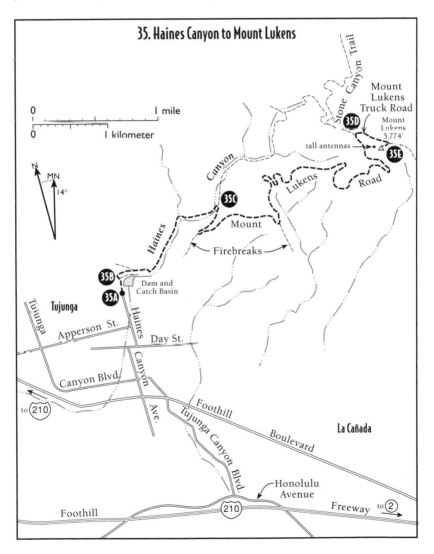

Haines Canyon (Photo by Jim Wolff)

SIGNIFICANT TRAIL LANDMARKS

35A. Trailhead on the right side of a gate.

35B. Take the left fork as you pass the reservoir.

35C. Intersection with the Mount Lukens Fire Road. Turn right onto road.

35D. End of fire road. Turn right onto Mount Lukens Truck Road.

35E. Summit of Mount Lukens marked by several antennas. Turn around and return to the start the same way you came.

36

Strawberry Peak

Distance: 10.2 miles

Course geometry: Point to point

Running time: 2–3.5 hours

Start altitude: 4,580 feet

Finish altitude: 3,670 feet

Elevation gain: 1,900 feet

Highest altitude: 5,300 feet

Difficulty: Strenuous

Water: At the start

Area management: Angeles National Forest

Maps: Condor Peak and Chilao Flat (USGS)
Trail Map of the Angeles Front Country

Beginning at nearly 4,600 feet in the scenic Angeles National Forest near Mount Wilson, this course wraps around magnificent mountain slopes. The sunnier ridges host yucca and cactus, while the shaded areas shelter moss

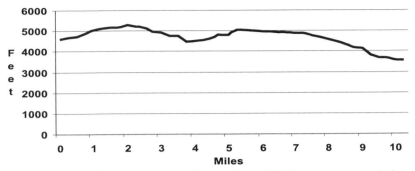

and pine trees. A fragrant sage meadow in the saddle between two peaks has pine trees with enormous cones. The enormous rock face of Strawberry Peak towers above. Along the way, there are occasional narrow and precipitous trails, expanses of pine forests, large granite boulders, and numerous stream crossings. The final few miles descend along wide switchbacks.

GETTING THERE

From the Foothill Freeway (Interstate 210), exit on the Angeles Crest Highway (State Highway 2) and drive north to Clear Creek Ranger Station at the intersection of Angeles Crest Highway and Angeles Forest Highway. Leave one car in the parking lot on the south side of the road or in the dirt parking area on the northeast corner.

Take the second car and continue east on Angeles Crest Highway to Red Box Ranger Station at the intersection with Mount Wilson Road. Drive into the parking lot on the south side of the road and park. The trailhead is across the road and slightly east. Parking requires an Adventure Pass.

THE RUN

Cross the Angeles Crest Highway, watching carefully for traffic, and head northeast. The trailhead (36A) is on the left just around the bend in the road 200 yards from the parking area. Run uphill and through a shallow canyon to a ridge. Avoid a trail leading to the right on the way up. At the ridge, another small trail leads to the left (36B); pass it and continue straight up the hill along the side of the mountain. Enjoy the wonderful mountain views.

At mile 2.3, you will reach a low saddle on the ridge between Strawberry Peak and Mount Lawlor (36C). A trail on the left continues up the ridge, but you stay on the trail to the right leading north into the canyon. For the next 1.8 miles, the trail is downhill along a rocky trail surrounded by numerous cactus and yuccas. Excellent views along the entire San Gabriel Range make

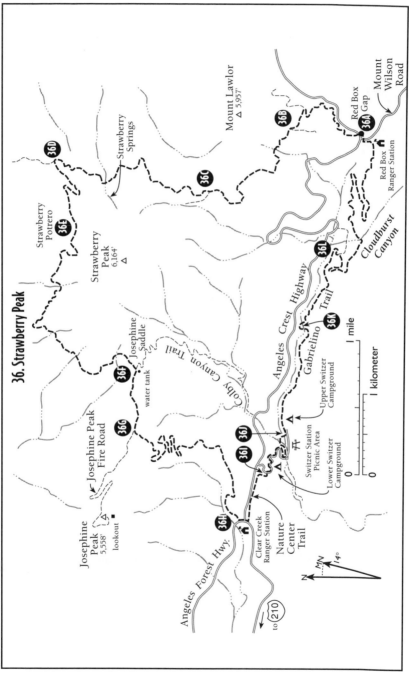

36. Strawberry Peak

Mount Wilson Road

Red Box Gap

Mount Lawlor
△ 5,957'

Red Box
Ranger Station

Strawberry
Springs

Cloudburst
Canyon

Strawberry
Potrero

Strawberry Peak
6,164'
△

Gabrielino Trail

Josephine
Saddle

water tank

Colby Canyon Trail

Angeles Crest Highway

Upper Switzer
Campground

1 mile

1 kilometer

Josephine Peak
Fire Road

Switzer Station
Picnic Area

Lower Switzer
Campground

0

0

Josephine
Peak
5,558'

lookout

Angeles Forest Hwy.

Clear Creek
Ranger Station

Nature
Center
Trail

MN
14°

N

to 210

this a particularly beautiful section. A sharp left turn marks the beginning of the trail leading to Strawberry Potrero (36D). The Strawberry Peak Trail leads to the right; you continue to the left heading west.

Follow this trail uphill along a streambed. The sandy trail leads to a wide, flat meadow (36E) with a large granite boulder near the middle. Aim toward the boulder and continue on the trail heading west. This area has picnic tables under the surrounding pine trees. The trail goes back uphill on the other side of the meadow.

The next 3.2 miles are cool and shaded by a pine and oak forest. As the trail climbs through small canyons, it eventually begins to level out, making it especially great for running. After rounding Strawberry Peak, the trail turns south and begins a gentle descent to Josephine Saddle (36F). There is a water tank here and an intersection with the Colby Canyon Trail going left steeply downhill. Continue to the right 0.5 mile to where the narrow trail ends at the Josephine Peak Fire Road (36G).

Turn left and follow the fire road down a series of steep switchbacks 2.4 miles to Angeles Forest Highway (36H). Turn left on Angeles Forest Highway and go one block south to the intersection with Angles Crest Highway and your car.

Option: If only one car is available or if a longer run is desired, when you reach the intersection of Angeles Forest Highway and Angeles Crest Highway (36H), you can return to Red Box Ranger Station on the Gabrielino Trail via Switzer Station Picnic Area.

Taking care to watch for traffic, cross Angeles Crest Highway and turn left toward the Clear Creek Ranger Station and parking area. From the northeast end of the parking area, go left onto the Nature Center Trail, which parallels the roadway on the south side. This trail ends in 0.5 mile at the road (36I) leading down to Switzer Station Picnic Area. At the road, turn right and descend the steep hill into the canyon. Switzer Station Picnic Area has restrooms, water, picnic areas, and campgrounds. Tall sycamore and pine trees along a stream provide abundant shade. This is a great spot to take a well-deserved break.

Follow the paved road through the parking area to where it ends at a stream crossing (36J) and continue east on the Gabrielino Trail. The trail follows the canyon uphill on the south side of the stream. The trail crosses the stream (36K) and immediately crosses back to the south side and continues east. After a sharp right turn (36L), the trail climbs out of the canyon on a series of switchbacks through sage scrub and oaks. This section of trail is particularly rocky. The trail ends at Red Box Ranger Station where you began. Congratulate yourself on completing this challenging run.

Strawberry Peak (Photo by Jim Wolff)

SIGNIFICANT TRAIL LANDMARKS

36A. Trailhead 200 yards northeast of the parking area.

36B. At the ridge, a trail intersects from the left. Continue straight uphill.

36C. At the saddle, stay on the trail to the right heading north into the canyon.

36D. Intersection with the Strawberry Peak Trail on the right. Take the sharp left turn leading to Strawberry Potrero.

36E. Enter a flat meadow, aim toward a large boulder, and continue on the trail heading west.

36F. Josephine Saddle and intersection with the Colby Canyon Trail on the left. Continue to the right.

36G. Trail ends at a fire road. Turn left and head downhill.

36H. Fire road ends at Angeles Forest Highway. Turn left and continue to the intersection with Angeles Crest Highway. Return to your car, or for the optional route back to Red Box Ranger Station, cross Angeles Crest Highway and turn left onto the Nature Center Trail.

36I. Nature Center Trail ends at paved road to Switzer Station Picnic Area. Turn right onto road.

36J. Switzer Road ends at a stream crossing. Continue east on the Gabrielino Trail.

36K. Stream crossing.

36L. Sharp right turn. Switchbacks lead out of canyon back to Red Box Ranger Station.

37
Santa Anita Canyon/Upper Winter Creek Loop

Distance: 8 miles
Course geometry: Loop
Running time: 1.5–2.5 hours
Start altitude: 2,170 feet
Finish altitude: 2,170 feet
Elevation gain: 2,340 feet
Highest altitude: 3,612 feet
Difficulty: Moderate
Water: At the start
Area management: Angeles National Forest
Maps: Mount Wilson and Azusa (USGS)
     Trail Map of the Angeles Front Country
     Trail Map for Trails of the Angeles

This excellent course has the excitement of waterfalls, forest, chaparral, and great views. Numerous signs along the well-maintained trail make it easy to stay on track. There are several restrooms, picnic areas, and campgrounds along the way. The trailhead is only a short drive from the Foothill Freeway (Interstate 210) near the greater Los Angeles area.

GETTING THERE
    From the Foothill Freeway (Interstate 210) in Sierra Madre, exit on Santa Anita Avenue and drive north. Santa Anita Avenue turns into Santa Anita Canyon Road as it begins climbing the twisting road to the Chantry Flat Picnic Area 5 miles from the freeway. Parking requires an Adventure Pass.

THE RUN
    The trailhead (37A) is on the right side of the road near the entrance to the parking area. The first 0.8 mile drops 400 feet into the canyon on an asphalt road. Halfway down, the road crosses Winter Creek where the Lower Winter Creek Trail ends on the left. Continue on the road into the canyon. The road ends (37B) and turns into a wide dirt trail following Santa Anita Creek. Tall aspens and oaks fill this beautiful canyon and large granite boulders line the streambed.

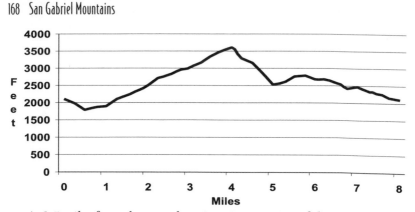

At 1.5 miles from the start there is an intersection of three trails (37C). The trail to the right follows the creek for 0.5 mile where it dead-ends at the bottom of Sturtevant Falls. If you want to see the falls, take the trail that crosses the stream, avoiding the private cabins on the left. Spend some time at the wonderful falls, which are about 50 feet high and spill over a shear, mossy cliff into a large pool. Relax and enjoy the sound of falling water.

The two other trails at the intersection lead to the left. The Upper Trail is for horses and the Lower Trail is for pedestrians. Both trails eventually lead to the same location higher in the canyon above Sturtevant Falls. Take the Lower Trail and climb up the side of the canyon. You can hear the falls as you get closer, and you can see it from the edge of a cliff (watch your footing carefully). Above the falls, the trail is carved out of the granite gorge. Inviting pools and a smaller waterfall are visible below.

At Falling Sign Junction, which is the intersection with the Upper Trail (37D), turn right and continue up the canyon to Cascade Picnic Area, where there is a restroom. Continue up the canyon to Spruce Grove Campground 4 miles from the start.

Just past Spruce Grove Campground, the Gabrielino Trail intersects on the right. Take this trail straight up the hill; it then turns left and leads back down to the stream. Cross the stream above a dam, and turn left onto the Mount Zion Trail at the Mount Zion Trail Junction (37E). Climb up Mount Zion Trail 1.25 miles to Mount Zion. Although the first 0.25 mile is a bit steep, the trail then levels out, rewarding you with excellent running along a smooth trail through spruce, oak, and bay trees. A small trail on the left (37F) goes 0.1 mile through manzanita to the 3,575-foot summit of Mount Zion. After claiming the summit, return to the Mount Zion Trail and turn left, descending into Winter Creek Canyon toward Hoegee Campground.

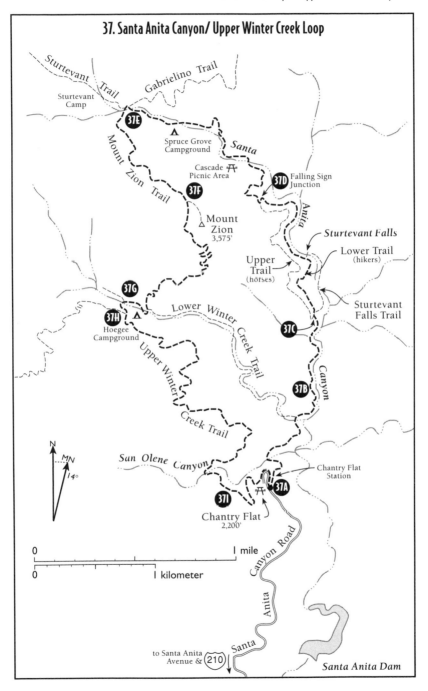

37. Santa Anita Canyon/ Upper Winter Creek Loop

Sturtevant Trail

Gabrielino Trail

Sturtevant Camp

37E

Spruce Grove Campground

Santa

Cascade Picnic Area

37F

Falling Sign Junction

37D

Mount Zion Trail

Mount Zion 3,575'

Sturtevant Falls

Lower Trail (hikers)

Upper Trail (horses)

37G

Anita

Sturtevant Falls Trail

Lower Winter Creek Trail

37H

Hoegee Campground

37C

Upper Winter Creek Trail

37B

Canyon

N

MN

14°

San Olene Canyon

Chantry Flat Station

37A

37I

Chantry Flat 2,200'

0 _____ 1 mile

0 _____ 1 kilometer

Canyon Road

Santa Anita

to Santa Anita Avenue & (210)

Santa

Santa Anita Dam

Santa Anita Canyon (Photo by Willy Blumhoff)

Follow a series of long switchbacks through the chaparral, taking care to avoid any low branches. As the trail reaches Winter Creek there is a sign marking the Lower Zion Trail Junction (37G). The trail to the left heading downstream is the Lower Winter Creek Trail, which leads to Chantry Flat in 2 miles. Continue on the trail to the right leading to the Upper Winter Creek Trail.

Just over a short hill there is an unmarked trail leading upstream. Do not take this trail. Instead cross to the left side of the stream and at the Upper Winter Creek Junction (37H), go left 3 miles to Chantry Flat. This excellent trail goes through a forest that winds along the contours of the steep mountainside. The trail ends at an asphalt road above Chantry Flat (37I). Turn left and go back to the parking area.

SIGNIFICANT TRAIL LANDMARKS
37A. Trailhead on right side of road near entrance to parking area.
37B. Paved road becomes a wide trail along Santa Anita Creek.
37C. Three-way intersection of Upper Trail, Lower Trail, and Sturtevant Falls Trail. Take the Lower Trail to the left.
37D. Falling Sign Junction. Turn right.
37E. Spruce Grove Campground and intersection with Gabrielino Trail. Turn right onto trail heading uphill. Cross stream and turn left at Mount Zion Trail Junction onto Mount Zion Trail.
37F. Intersection with Mount Zion Summit Trail.
37G. Lower Zion Trail Junction, turn right.
37H. Cross over to left side of stream. At Upper Winter Creek Trail Junction, turn left.
37I. Trail ends at paved road. Turn left to return to parking lot.

38
Shortcut Canyon

Distance: 8.8 miles
Course geometry: Out and back
Running time: 1.5–3 hours
Start altitude: 4,700 feet
Finish altitude: 4,700 feet
Elevation gain: 1,700 feet
Highest altitude: 4,700 feet
Difficulty: Strenuous
Water: None
Area management: Angeles National Forest
Maps: Mount Wilson and Chilao Flat (USGS)
   Trail Map of the Angeles Front Country
   Trail Map for Trails of the Angeles

This great canyon course is located north of Mount Wilson and leads down to the west fork of the San Gabriel River. The upper sections of trail are exposed. The lower sections follow a tranquil, boulder-filled stream shaded by oak and pine trees. This is a wonderfully rejuvenating escape from the city.

GETTING THERE
   From the Foothill Freeway (Interstate 210), exit on the Angeles Crest Highway (State Highway 2) and drive north 18 miles to the Shortcut parking area. Park in the wide area on the north side of the road. Parking requires an Adventure Pass.

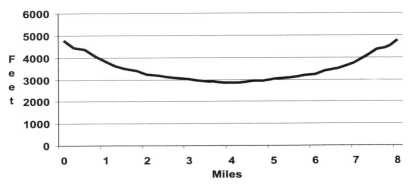

THE RUN

A small post marks the trailhead (38A) directly across the road to the south. The trail begins down a series of steep switchbacks leading to a fire road (38B). Turn right on the fire road and look for a small trail marker 100 yards up on the left side (38C). Turn left and descend into Shortcut Canyon on the Silver Moccasin Trail along several longer switchbacks through sage scrub, watching out for loose rocks and dead yucca stalks on the trail.

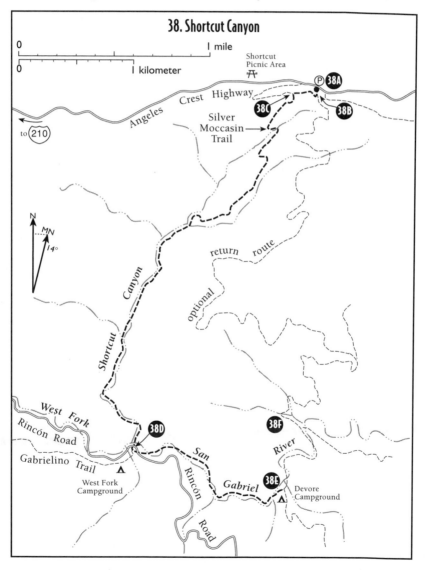

After the first of many stream crossings, the trail becomes shaded and follows the contours of the hillsides. Be alert for large patches of poison oak in the canyon. A dense mat of leaves, pinecones, and acorns carpets the trail in early spring. There are no trail markers, so take care when crossing the stream to ensure you pick up the trail again.

In 3.3 miles, the trail goes to West Fork Campground (38D), which has tables and a rustic restroom. The Rincón Road and the Gabrielino Trail both intersect at West Fork Campground. Turn right on the Gabrielino Trail and follow it east along the river to where it becomes the west fork of the San Gabriel River.

Cross the river and in 1.1 miles you will come to the Devore Campground (38E). The turnaround point is on the right bank. Spend some time in the canyon and enjoy the peaceful atmosphere before turning back the way you came.

Option: An adventurous option is to continue along the river from Devore Campground for another 0.5 mile. Pick up the trail on the north side of the river. It will soon disappear, leaving you to find the best path. The canyon narrows and the rocky banks are covered with large patches of poison oak. If the water is not too cold or too high and swift, avoid the poison oak by walking through the river, but watch out for flash floods in the summer.

In the last portion of this section, the trail is on the left side of the river

Stream crossing in Shortcut Canyon (Photo by Jim Wolff)

and ends at a fire road. Turn left onto the fire road (38F) to return to the start on the road, or turn around and return to the start the way you came. If you take the fire road, avoid any other roads leading to the right. The fire road has great views of Mount Wilson, San Gabriel Canyon, and Mount Baldy. As you approach the top of the fire road near Angeles Crest Highway, turn right on the narrow trail to return to the start.

SIGNIFICANT TRAIL LANDMARKS
38A. Trailhead on south side of Angeles Crest Highway.
38B. Intersection with fire road. Turn right.
38C. Look for trail marker indicating the Silver Moccasin Trail on left. Turn left onto trail.
38D. West Fork Campground. Turn left on Gabrielino Trail heading east.
38E. Devore Campground; the turnaround point is on the right bank of the river.
38F. On optional course, follow trail along river to fire road on left bank. Turn left onto fire road and return to the start on the fire road, or turn around to return on the Silver Moccasin Trail.

39
Chilao Flat

Distance: 6.5 miles
Course geometry: Out and back
Running time: 1.1–1.7 hours
Start altitude: 5,300 feet
Finish altitude: 5,300 feet
Elevation gain: 1,000 feet
Highest altitude: 6,000 feet
Difficulty: Moderate
Water: In Chilao Campground and Charlton Flats
Area management: Angeles National Forest
Maps: Chilao Flat (USGS)
  Trail Map of the Angeles Front Country
  Trail Map for Trails of the Angeles

This course offers a great view from the summit of Mount Vetter. It has only one moderate climb, but the altitude makes it challenging. The run starts in

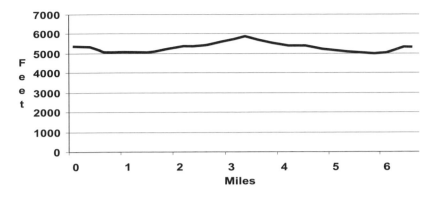

sage scrub and then follows a streambed under tall pine trees to Charlton Flats. The climb to Mount Vetter takes you along a sandy, manzanita-covered hillside.

GETTING THERE

From the Foothill Freeway (Interstate 210), exit on the Angeles Crest Highway (State Highway 2) and drive north 23 miles to the entrance to Chilao Campground. Turn left into the campground. The trailhead is on the left where the road forks 280 yards from the turn. Parking requires an Adventure Pass.

THE RUN

The trailhead (39A), located on the left 280 yards from the turn into Chilao Campground, is marked with a signpost. Follow the narrow trail up a short hill through manzanita bushes. As it rounds the top of the hill, several intersecting trails lead to the campground. Follow the trail markers leading down a rocky section to a stream crossing. The trail turns south, ending at a wide fire road (39B) alongside a stream. Turn left onto the fire road and follow it through pine and oak forests as the road pursues the stream.

At mile 1.5, the trail crosses to the right side of the stream (39C) and goes uphill. At the top of the hill, the trail crosses a paved road (39D) at the north end of Charlton Flats Picnic Grounds. A trail marker on the other side of the road indicates where the trail picks up again. This narrow trail turns to the southwest between two paved roads following a streambed.

The trail crosses two more paved roads (39E and 39F) as it climbs away from the Charlton Flats Picnic Grounds. After the second road crossing, the trail follows a small stream west in a shallow gully under oak trees and through chaparral. The final section to the summit has several short, steep switchbacks ending at a fire road just below the Mount Vetter summit (39G).

Follow the fire road up to the 5,908-foot summit and a historic overlook structure with fantastic views in all directions. Observe Mount Wilson and Shortcut Saddle. Distant peaks within the San Gabriel Range are visible. This

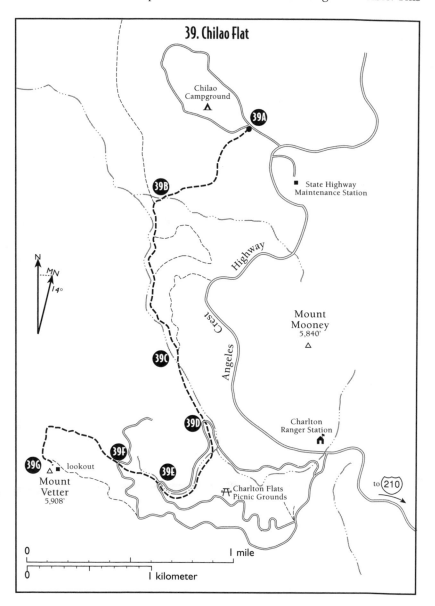

39. Chilao Flat

Chilao Campground

State Highway Maintenance Station

Highway

N
MN
14°

Mount Mooney
5,840'

Angeles Crest

Charlton Ranger Station

lookout

Mount Vetter
5,908'

Charlton Flats Picnic Grounds

to 210

0   1 mile
0   1 kilometer

Pinecones (Photo by Jim Wolff)

is a wonderful spot to enjoy a hard-earned break after capturing the summit. Return to the start the way you came.

Option: If you have two cars, a point-to-point run is possible. Leave one car at the start and one at Charlton Flats. To get to Charlton Flats from Chilao by car, drive south on the Angeles Crest Highway (State Highway 2) approximately 3 miles and turn right onto the road leading to Charlton Flats. When you enter Charlton Flats, take the road to the left, avoiding all other roads leading to the right, and follow it until it ends at a fire road. This fire road goes 0.75 mile up to the summit of Mount Vetter.

Another one-way option is to reverse the run by starting in Charlton Flats.

SIGNIFICANT TRAIL LANDMARKS

39A. Trailhead marked with signpost.

39B. Intersection with wide fire road. Turn left onto road.

39C. Stream crossing. Continue uphill on the right side of the stream.

39D. Fire road crosses paved road at north end of Charlton Flats Picnic Grounds. Trail marker on opposite side of road.

39E. Trail crosses paved road. Continue straight ahead across road.

39F. Trail crosses paved road. Continue straight ahead across road.

39G. Intersection with fire road below Mount Vetter summit. Follow the fire road to the historic overlook. Return to the start the way you came.

40

Cooper Canyon

Distance: 13.6 miles
Course geometry: Out and back
Running time: 2.3–3.4 hours
Start altitude: 7,000 feet
Finish altitude: 7,000 feet
Elevation gain: 2,818 feet
Highest altitude: 7,000 feet
Difficulty: Strenuous
Water: None
Area management: Angeles National Forest
Maps: Waterman Mountain (USGS)
  Trail Map of the Angeles Front Country
  Trail Map for Trails of the Angeles

This course begins at 7,000 feet with a wonderful descent into Cooper Canyon. The well-maintained trail traverses steep slopes covered with pine forests and manzanita groves. On the canyon floor, the trail follows a wonderful stream filled with huge granite boulders. Two formidable climbs provide awesome views of the canyon and surrounding areas.

GETTING THERE

From the Foothill Freeway (Interstate 210), exit on the Angeles Crest Highway (State Highway 2) and drive north 26 miles to the Cloudburst Summit parking area. Park in the wide area on the north side of the road. Parking requires an Adventure Pass.

THE RUN

The trailhead (40A) is located on the east side of a fire road that leads north downhill from the parking area. The trail rapidly descends a steep slope on switchbacks and then levels out near a streambed and continues northeast. At an intersection with the fire road (40B), cross the road to where a sign marks the trail leading to the right. Follow it uphill and around a small canyon. At another trail marker (40C), turn right into Cooper Canyon where the trail is smooth and easy to run on.

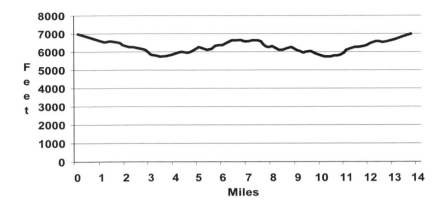

A sign marks the Cooper Canyon Campground (40D) as you approach a stream. Rustic toilet facilities are available on the other side of the stream. Continue east downstream as the trail leads downhill through the heart of the canyon lush with beautiful, shady pine and redwood trees.

The trail crosses the stream and intersects with the south fork of the Burkhart Trail (40E) at the top of a short hill. This trail leads 1.4 miles up to Buckhorn Flat Campground near Angles Crest Highway. Pass the Burkhart Trail and continue downstream past a sheer rock cliff. Cross the stream to reach an intersection with the north fork of the Burkhart Trail to the left and the Rattlesnake Trail to the right (40F).

Take the Rattlesnake Trail, which follows the stream and then goes left through a small canyon. Continue to climb following the contour of the hillside. Several sections of this trail are almost level and provide some great running. A short downhill section leads to another stream crossing (40G) and marks the final leg leading out of Cooper Canyon.

As you climb out of the steep canyon, take the time to look at the huge rock formations that tower over the canyon to the northeast, making it look like a miniature Yosemite Valley. The last 0.5 mile leads northeast and ends at Angeles Crest Highway. Directly across the roadway is Eagles Roost Picnic Area (40H) with restrooms near the parking area. Take a break and then return to the start the way you came.

Option: If two cars are available, a point-to-point run is possible. Leave one car at Eagles Roost, which is 4.5 miles east of the Cloudburst Summit parking area. Starting in either direction is possible. Another option is to do an out-and-back run to the middle of the canyon near the Burkhart Trail starting from either Cloudburst Summit or Eagles Roost.

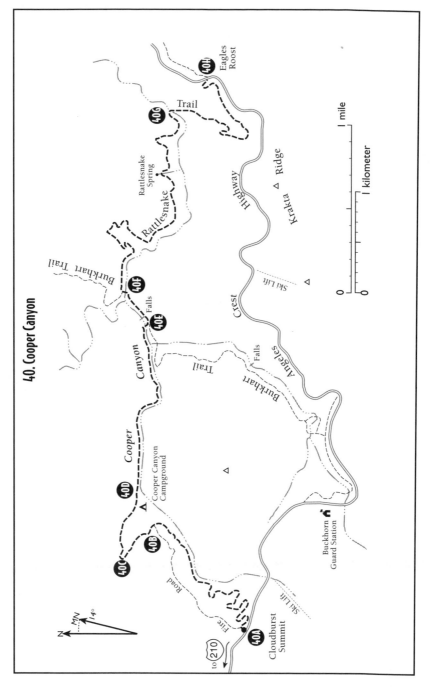

40. Cooper Canyon

SIGNIFICANT TRAIL LANDMARKS

40A. Trailhead on east side of fire road.

40B. Intersection with fire road. Cross road to trail marker and continue to the right.

40C. Trail marker and right turn into Cooper Canyon.

40D. Cooper Canyon Campground.

40E. Stream crossing and intersection with the south fork of the Burkhart Trail. Continue downstream past rock cliff.

40F. Intersection with north fork of Burkhart Trail and Rattlesnake Trail. Take the Rattlesnake Trail to the right.

40G. Downhill section leads to stream crossing.

40H. Eagles Roost Picnic Area. Return to the start on the same course.

A snowy Cooper Canyon Trail (Photo by Jim Wolff)

JOSHUA TREE NATIONAL MONUMENT
Twentynine Palms, Palm Springs

The Joshua Tree National Monument is located on the border between the Mojave and Colorado Deserts east of Los Angeles. This exceptional area is famous for the indigenous Joshua trees and interesting rock formations popular with rock climbers around the world. The worn desert lands are exposed to the elements of wind, water, and heat. Being equally exposed, visitors must carefully plan their trail running excursions into this wonderful wilderness.

While trail running in the Joshua Tree National Monument, you may feel as if you are a visitor in another world. The character of the region unfolds around every turn in sand and stone sculptures that are highlighted with muted gray-green plants, sometimes blossoming with brilliant colors and startling shapes.

41

Boy Scout Trail

Distance: 15.6 miles
Course geometry: Out and back
Running time: 2.5–4.5 hours
Start altitude: 2,840 feet
Finish altitude: 2,840 feet
Elevation gain: 1,570 feet
Highest altitude: 4,160 feet
Difficulty: Moderate
Water: None
Area management: Joshua Tree National Park
Maps: Joshua Tree (USGS)
   Recreation Map of Joshua Tree National Park

Joshua Tree National Park is a magical place guaranteed to inspire visitors with its beauty. The landscape reflects the ever-changing desert light with a kaleidoscope of color. Trails meander through twisting canyons filled with sand, boulders, and desert flora. Statuesque Joshua trees stand like sentries under deep blue skies, offering their outstretched limbs in welcome to all.

In mild weather, this 16-mile, out-and-back run is challenging. In warmer weather, you can run it as an 8-mile, point-to-point run. Beware that summer temperatures and humidity can make running in this area hazardous. Water can be stored at a parking area near the turnaround point, but remember to

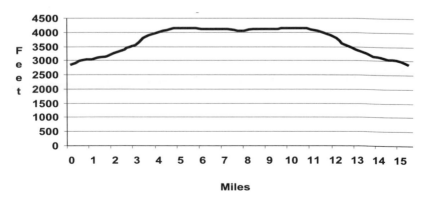

take all trash out with you. The trail is well marked with unobtrusive wooden signposts, but carry a map and compass to avoid getting lost. Be sure to check the local weather conditions for flash-flood warnings. Park entry is $10 per car.

GETTING THERE

From Los Angeles, take the San Bernardino Freeway (Interstate 10) east to Highway 62 and turn north. Drive 40 miles to the main entrance to the park. From Highway 62 (also known as Twentynine Palms Highway), turn right onto Indian Cove Road. The trailhead (41A) is located on the right 0.5 mile past the Indian Cove Ranger Station. Park in the wide turnout at the trailhead.

THE RUN

The Boy Scout Trail begins with a gradual uphill climb across the open desert and heads toward the rocky hills 1.5 miles away. Cross a narrow gully at mile 0.5 (41B). As you approach the hills, the trail follows a narrow canyon along the streambed. The soft, sandy soil provides a comfortable surface for running. Take time to notice all the varieties of cactus and the numerous Joshua trees.

At the end of the first section of canyon, the trail climbs a series of short switchbacks leading to a ridge (41C) at mile 2. There are great views north toward Twentynine Palms. For the next 3 miles, the trail follows a sandy streambed through several small canyons. This section ends with a climb up to the left out of the streambed (41D).

The trail steadily gains altitude over the next 5 miles, then levels out as it leaves the canyons behind. The view opens across Hidden Valley to the eastern end of the San Bernardino Mountains. Several isolated rock formations punctuate the desert floor covered with sage, cactus, and Joshua trees.

At 7 miles, the Willow Hole Trail leads away to the left (41E). Continue south on the Boy Scout Trail. The trail soon jogs to the right (41F) to avoid an area closed for ecological restoration. Watch for signs advising you to stay out of sensitive areas. At mile 7.8, the trail ends at Park Boulevard (41G), where there is a small parking area. This is the turnaround point. Take some time to explore the nearby rock formations and enjoy a break in their shade. Return to the start the way you came.

Option: If two cars are available, this course can be run from point to point in either direction. Another option is to reverse the out-and-back course, running from 41G to 41A.

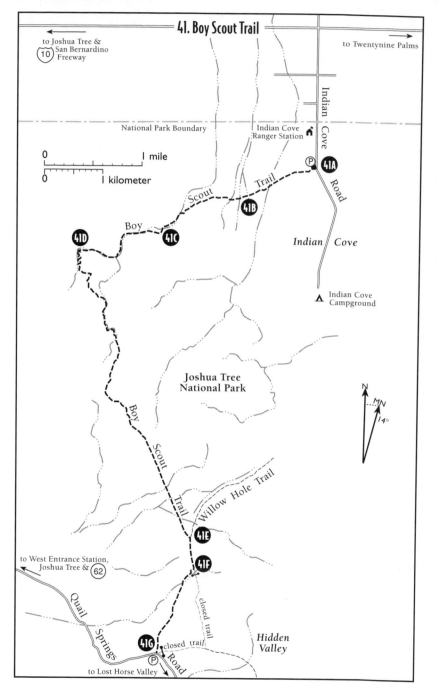

41. Boy Scout Trail

to Joshua Tree &
San Bernardino
Freeway

to Twentynine Palms

National Park Boundary

Indian Cove
Ranger Station

0   1 mile
0   1 kilometer

Boy   Scout   Trail

41A

41B

41C

41D

Indian   Cove

Indian Cove
Campground

Joshua Tree
National Park

Boy

Scout

Trail

Willow Hole Trail

41E

41F

to West Entrance Station,
Joshua Tree & 62

Quail   Springs

closed trail

41G

closed trail

Hidden
Valley

to Lost Horse Valley

Road

N
MN
14°

Boy Scout Trail

SIGNIFICANT TRAIL LANDMARKS

41A. Trailhead on right 0.5 mile past Indian Cove Ranger Station.

41B. Cross a narrow gully at mile 0.5.

41C. Climb short switchbacks to a ridge.

41D. Climb out of the streambed to the left.

41E. Intersection with Willow Hole Trail at mile 7. Continue south.

41F. Trail jogs to the right around an ecological restoration area.

41G. Park Boulevard. Turnaround point; return to the start the way you came.

ORANGE AND SAN DIEGO COUNTIES

Laguna Beach, Irvine, Santa Ana,
Anaheim, San Diego, El Cajon, Escondido

From the coastal San Joaquin Hills near Laguna Beach and Irvine, to the Laguna Mountains in the Cleveland National Forest, to beaches near Torrey Pines, Orange and San Diego Counties offer an extraordinary variety of trails. These trails take you though areas of historical significance for native people and for the national and state heritage of Mexico and California. Several of these areas are close to Los Angeles.

The Laguna Mountains have many of the highest peaks in San Diego County. This region has wonderful forests and streams and separates the San Diego area from the Anza Borrego Desert to the east. The mountain trails are close to Los Angeles and are a terrific destination for spending time in the coastal towns of Laguna Beach and Newport Beach.

San Diego's temperate climate makes it ideal for recreation and especially for trail running.

42

Aliso and Wood Canyon Wilderness Park

Distance: 8.5 miles

Course geometry: Out-and-back loop

Running time: 1.25–2.5 hours

Start altitude: 1,010 feet

Finish altitude: 1,010 feet

Elevation gain: 1,800 feet

Highest altitude: 1,010 feet

Difficulty: Moderate

Water: At the start and finish

Area management: Orange County Harbors, Beaches and Parks
  City of Laguna Beach
  County of Orange Public Facilities Resources Department

Maps: San Juan Capistrano (USGS)

Delightful plants including wild artichokes, cactus, and colorful flowers line this course in abundance. A tree-lined stream is at the bottom of Wood Canyon. Rabbits are plentiful and often dart across the trail as you approach. The challenging climbs will get your heart pumping. The public park at the trailhead has restrooms, water, tennis courts, a playground, and a community center. Dogs are not allowed in county parks.

GETTING THERE

From the intersection of Laguna Canyon Road and Pacific Coast Highway, drive south and turn left on Forest Avenue. Drive one block and turn right, then turn left on Park Avenue. Take Park Avenue uphill through residential areas for 2.5 miles and turn left on Alta Laguna Road. Continue to Laguna Park and park free in the city lot or on the street.

THE RUN

The trail begins at the northwest corner of the parking lot (42A). The trail from the parking lot intersects with the wide West Ridge Trail (42B) 100 yards down. Turn right onto the trail. There are great views of Laguna Canyon to

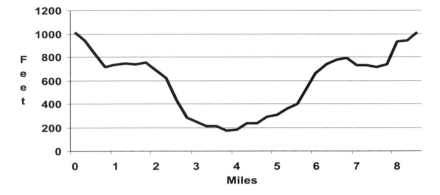

the left and Wood Canyon to the right as the trail descends to an intersection with the Mathis Canyon Trail (42C) leading to the right.

Continue on the West Ridge Trail to the left. One mile farther on, just before a large water tank and radio tower, turn right onto the Rock-It Trail (42D). This smooth trail goes through coastal sage scrub with wild artichokes growing abundantly on the hillsides. The trail passes under large powerlines in the upper section (42E).

The 1.5-mile Rock-It Trail leads to the Coyote Run Trail (42F). At the fork, go right and follow the trail down Wood Canyon to the south. Ignore unauthorized trails leading to the left (42G). The trail follows the stream and leads to an intersection with the lower Mathis Canyon Trail (42H). Continue to the left and cross the stream at the concrete culvert. After crossing the stream, turn left at the bulletin board onto the Wood Canyon Trail (42I).

The wide trail follows the stream up the canyon through an open field. Reforestation efforts are underway in this area, but it will be some time before runners reap the benefits of this program. You will pass the old Sheep Corral, a historic landmark of the Moulton family ranch. An information plaque details its historic significance. Pass the Five Oaks Trail (42J) on the right and continue on the Wood Canyon Trail.

The trail gradually climbs up a canyon filled with oak and sycamore trees. One mile from the Sheep Corral, the Coyote Run Trail (42K) intersects on the left. Continue straight ahead, passing the Lynx Trail (42L) on the left. Continue straight ahead. As the trail rises higher out of the canyon, the Cholla Trail (42M) intersects from the left and the Wood Canyon Trail ends just beyond this intersection in a housing tract. Take the Cholla Trail uphill to the left through sage and cactus. In 0.25 mile, it ends at the West Ridge Trail (42N). Turn left, passing the Lynx Trail (42O), and continuing past the water tank (42D) to retrace your steps to the start.

SIGNIFICANT TRAIL LANDMARKS

42A. Trailhead at northwest corner of parking lot.

42B. Intersection with West Ridge Trail. Turn right onto trail.

42C. Intersection with the Mathis Canyon Trail. Continue left.

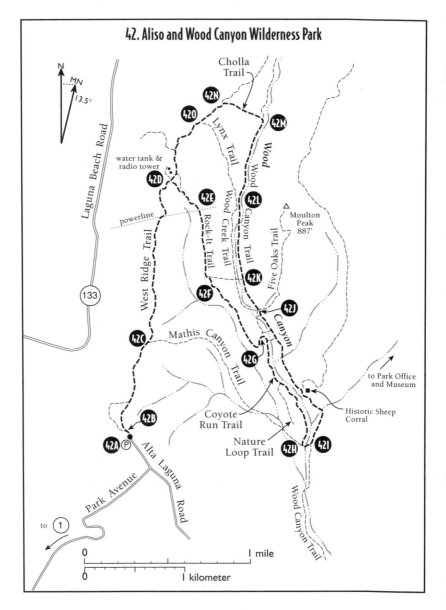

42. Aliso and Wood Canyon Wilderness Park

Coyote Run Trail (Photo by Stan Swartz)

42D. Intersection with the Rock-It Trail near water tank and radio tower. Turn right onto trail.

42E. Cross under large powerlines.

42F. Start of Coyote Run Trail. Go right onto trail at fork.

42G. Unauthorized trails to the left.

42H. Intersection with the Mathis Canyon Trail on right. Continue left.

42I. Stream crossing at culvert. Turn left onto the Wood Canyon Trail.

42J. Intersection with Five Oaks Trail on the right. Continue straight ahead.

42K. Pass the Coyote Run Trail on the left.

42L. Intersection with the Lynx Trail on the left. Continue straight ahead.

42M. Intersection with the Cholla Trail on the left. Turn left onto trail.

42N. End of Cholla Trail at intersection with West Ridge Trail. Turn left onto West Ridge Trail.

42O. Pass the Lynx Trail on the left.

43

El Moro Canyon

Distance: 9 miles
Course geometry: Loop
Running time: 1.5–2.5 hours
Start altitude: 125 feet
Finish altitude: 125 feet
Elevation gain: 1,300 feet
Highest altitude: 1,000 feet
Difficulty: Moderate
Water: At start and finish
Area management: Crystal Cove State Park
Maps: Laguna Beach (USGS)

Open fields of grass and wildflowers and sagebrush-covered hills with ocean and canyon views characterize this course. The descent into the canyon follows a stream with heavy vegetation. The parking area is at the ranger station with restrooms, water, and an information kiosk with free maps.

GETTING THERE

From Laguna Beach, drive north on Pacific Coast Highway and turn right at the entrance to El Moro Canyon parking area located just north of the entrance to the El Moro School. From Newport Beach, drive south on Pacific Coast Highway to the El Moro Canyon parking area and turn left. Drive up the short road to the parking lot. Parking is $6.

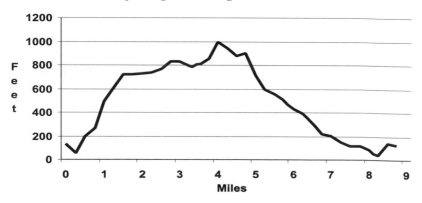

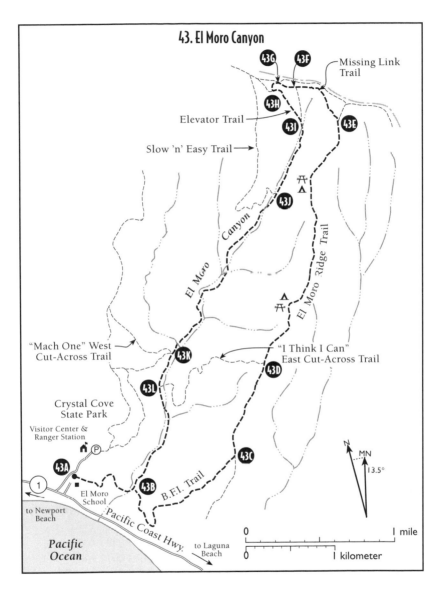

43. El Moro Canyon

43G 43F Missing Link Trail

43H

Elevator Trail

43I

Slow 'n' Easy Trail →

43E

El Moro Canyon

43J

El Moro Ridge Trail

"Mach One" West Cut-Across Trail

43K

"I Think I Can" East Cut-Across Trail

43D

43L

Crystal Cove State Park

Visitor Center & Ranger Station

43A

43C

1

El Moro School

43B B.F.I. Trail

to Newport Beach

Pacific Coast Hwy.

to Laguna Beach

Pacific Ocean

N MN 13.5°

0   1 mile

0   1 kilometer

THE RUN

The trail begins at a kiosk southwest of the parking lot (43A). The first 0.5 mile on a fire road passes behind the El Moro School and a trailer park. After the trail crosses a streambed, take the narrow B.F.I. Trail (43B) to the right up a small hill. It will intersect with the El Moro Ridge Trail (43C) and climb for the next mile over intermittent sections of asphalt, gravel, and dirt.

El Moro Ridge Trail

Grass and sage cover the hillsides and there are excellent views of Crystal Cove Beach and the surrounding area.

One mile up the El Moro Ridge Trail, the "I Think I Can" East Cut-Across Trail (43D) intersects on the left. Continue straight ahead on the El Moro Ridge Trail. In the next mile, two camping areas provide tables and chemical toilets. The views become increasingly dramatic as you run along on the ridge.

At 4.5 miles from the start, the Missing Link Trail (43E) intersects on the left. Turn onto this narrow, 0.5-mile trail leading north into El Moro Canyon. A short distance up the trail, the Missing Link Trail intersects with a wide, unnamed trail (43F); turn right to avoid an extremely steep portion of this unnamed trail to the left. Shortly after turning right on the unnamed trail, look for another narrow, unnamed trail on the left just before reaching a locked gate (43G). Take this narrow trail left and continue 100 yards down into the canyon to the Elevator Trail (43H). The short Elevator Trail soon joins the El Moro Canyon Trail (43I).

As you proceed down through the canyon, the Slow 'n' Easy Trail (43J) intersects from the right. Continue on the El Moro Canyon Trail. At 1.25 miles beyond the end of the Elevator Trail (43I), the Mach 1 and the West Cut-Across Trails (43K) intersect on the right. Continue straight to a fork in the trail (43L). The "I Think I Can" East Cut-Across Trail is on the left. Take the right fork and continue down the canyon under oak and sycamore trees. Many birds of prey may be seen circling the hilltops. The canyon trail is smooth, wide, and downhill. As you approach the end of the run, on your left you will pass the B.F.I. Trail you took on the way in. Continue past the trailer park and school and return to the start.

SIGNIFICANT TRAIL LANDMARKS

43A. Trailhead near kiosk southwest of parking lot.

43B. Intersection with the B.F.I. Trail. Turn right onto trail.

43C. Intersection with the El Moro Ridge Trail. Turn left onto trail.

43D. Intersection with the "I Think I Can" Trail. Continue straight ahead.

43E. Intersection with the Missing Link Trail. Turn left onto trail.

43F. Intersection with a wide, unnamed trail to the right. Turn right onto the wide trail.

43G. Fork in trail. Take the narrow, unnamed trail to the left.

43H. Intersection with the Elevator Trail. Turn left downhill on the Elevator Trail.

43I. Convergence of Elevator Trail with El Moro Canyon Trail.

43J. Intersection of the Slow 'n' Easy Trail from the right. Continue straight ahead.

43K. Intersection with the Mach 1 and West Cut-Across Trails. Continue straight ahead.

43L. Fork in trail at intersection with the "I Think I Can" East Cut-Across Trail. Take the right fork to return to the start.

44
Torrey Pines State Reserve

Distance: 4.5 miles

Course geometry: Loop

Running time: 0.75–1.5 hours

Start altitude: 45 feet

Finish altitude: 45 feet

Elevation gain: 570 feet

Highest altitude: 340 feet

Difficulty: Easy

Water: At the trailhead and along the course

Area management: California State Parks

Maps: La Jolla and Del Mar (USGS)

Torrey Pines State Reserve offers spectacular ocean and shoreline views from the top of weather-beaten cliffs. The smooth, sandy trails wind through native chaparral. Rare Torrey pines grow on ridges between deep canyons that

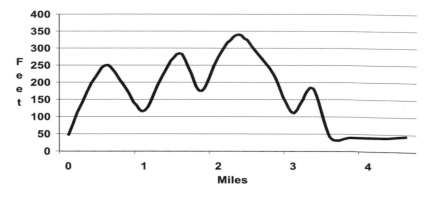

end at the sea. If the tide is low, running back to the parking lot on the beach adds additional exhilaration to an already extraordinary run. Several loop courses can be combined for a longer run amid the beautiful geological formations and rock outcroppings. The trails are narrow and can be busy on weekends, so it is best to run early in the morning. At high tide, waves crashing against the cliffs make beach running impossible, so plan accordingly.

GETTING THERE

From the San Diego Freeway (Interstate 5), exit on Carmel Valley Road and head west for 2 miles. At Pacific Coast Highway, turn left and drive south 1 mile across the Peñasquito Lagoon. Turn right into the driveway leading to a parking area at the base of the hill. Parking is $4. Note that Pacific Coast Highway becomes North Torrey Pines Road south of the parking area.

THE RUN

From the parking area (44A), proceed south up the paved road for 0.5 mile. After rounding a switchback and just past a small parking area, take the Guy Fleming Trail (44B), a relatively flat 0.75-mile loop.

When you return to the road, turn right and go 0.25 mile uphill to a right turn onto the Parry Grove Trail (44C). The Parry Grove Trail is a 0.5-mile loop with a native plant garden at the trailhead. The first part of the trail descends 100 steps from the main trail.

After returning to the road once more, turn right and go 0.25 mile uphill to the next parking area, which has a bulletin board with a helpful map (44D). The Torrey Pines Visitor Center and Ranger Station is directly across the street. Two trails begin west of the bulletin board, the Beach Trail to the left and the Razor Point Trail on the right. These trails are interconnected and

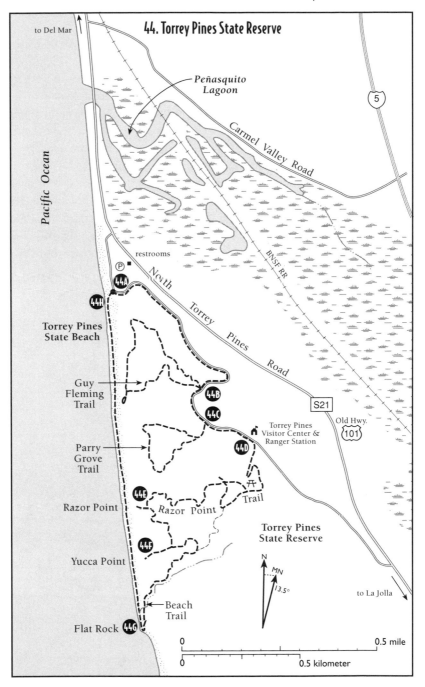

44. Torrey Pines State Reserve

to Del Mar

Peñasquito Lagoon

Carmel Valley Road

Pacific Ocean

BNSF RR

5

restrooms

P

44A

44H

Torrey Pines State Beach

Guy Fleming Trail

North Torrey Pines Road

44B

44C

S21

Old Hwy. 101

Torrey Pines Visitor Center & Ranger Station

Parry Grove Trail

44D

Razor Point

44E

Razor Point Trail

Torrey Pines State Reserve

Yucca Point

44F

N

MN

13.5°

to La Jolla

Beach Trail

Flat Rock 44G

0   0.5 mile

0   0.5 kilometer

lead to Razor Point, Yucca Point, and Flat Rock on the beach. Take the trail to Razor Point, return and take the combined trail to Yucca Point, then visit Flat Rock via the Beach Trail.

The distance to Razor Point is 0.7 mile, and the run has views of the surrealistic narrow canyons and steep red cliffs that characterize this area. The Beach Trail leads 0.7 mile to Flat Rock on the beach. The final section of this narrow trail is on a precipitous cliff face. The Razor Point and Beach Trails are connected at their west end by a trail leading to Yucca Point.

After descending to Razor Point on the Razor Point Trail (44E), return and take the combined trail to Yucca Point (44F). From there, follow signs to the Beach Trail. Take Beach Trail to Flat Rock (44G). If the tide is high, return to the start the way you came. If the tide is low, run north from Flat Rock along the beach for 1 mile and enjoy hard-packed sand, seagulls, and pounding surf. At the end of the cliffs (44H), exit the beach to the right and return to the parking lot.

SIGNIFICANT TRAIL LANDMARKS

44A. Trailhead at south end of parking lot. Proceed up the paved road.
44B. Guy Fleming Trail on the right. Turn right onto trail to make loop. Return to road and turn right.

Trail leading to Flat Rock

44C. Parry Grove Trail on the right. Turn right onto trail to make loop. Return to road and turn right.

44D. The Razor Point and Beach Trails are 0.25 mile from the Parry Grove Trail.

44E. Razor Point Trail.

44F. Yucca Point.

44G. Flat Rock.

44H. End of cliffs. Exit beach to the right to return to parking lot.

45

Los Peñasquitos Canyon Preserve

Distance: 12.5 miles
Course geometry: Out and back
Running time: 1.75–2.5 hours
Start altitude: 65 feet
Finish altitude: 65 feet
Elevation gain: 450 feet
Highest altitude: 300 feet
Difficulty: Easy
Water: At the eastern end of the canyon
Area management: Los Peñasquitos Canyon Preserve (LPCP)
Maps: Del Mar (USGS)

Peñasquitos translates from the Spanish as "little cliffs." The name references the steep hills that border this delightful canyon. This area includes land first granted to San Diego by Mexico in 1820. This course has several short,

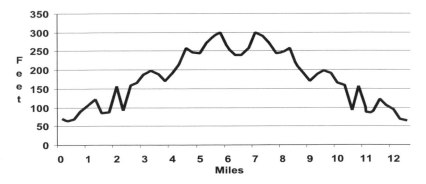

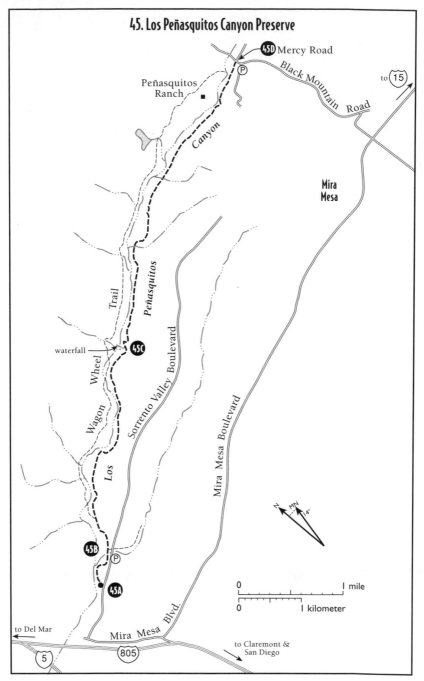

45. Los Peñasquitos Canyon Preserve

45D Mercy Road

Black Mountain Road

to 15

Peñasquitos Ranch

Canyon

Mira Mesa

Trail

Peñasquitos

Wheel

waterfall

45C

Sorrento Valley Boulevard

Wagon

Mira Mesa Boulevard

Los

45B

P

45A

N   MN
4°

0   1 mile

0   1 kilometer

to Del Mar

Mira Mesa Blvd.

to Claremont & San Diego

5   805

Los Peñasquitos Canyon

steep hills offering great workouts in a quiet canyon with abundant sycamore, eucalyptus, and oak trees. Midway up the canyon, a rock-filled gorge with a waterfall provides a great spot to rest. There are mile markers along the trails, which are shared by cyclists, hikers, and equestrians. Several historical structures in the canyon provide interesting background material about the area.

GETTING THERE

Heading north on Interstate 805, get off at Mira Mesa Boulevard and continue north through the traffic light on Vista Sorrento Parkway for 0.5 mile to Sorrento Valley Boulevard; turn right and continue for 1 mile. The trailhead is located 0.25 mile past the last building on the left side of the road. The parking area is about 0.25 mile farther up with restrooms and a secondary trailhead on the right.

THE RUN

The trailhead is located just off Sorrento Valley Boulevard through a gate (45A). You will see a historic adobe structure on the right. Continue on the single track for 0.5 mile to an intersection with a fire road (45B). Turn left onto the fire road. A stream parallels the entire trail as it meanders through groves of sycamore and coastal live oaks. At mile 2.75, a short trail on the left leads to a pleasant little waterfall (45C). After exploring the falls, return to the trail and continue east on the fire road. The turnaround point is at Black Mountain Road (45D), where there is a parking area, toilets, and a drinking fountain. Return to the start the way you came.

Option: If you are more adventurous, you can take the less traveled trails on the north side of the stream to return to the start. Cross the stream 0.25 mile from the end of the trail at Black Mountain Road and continue back on trails that parallel the stream leading west. Along the way, pass the Peñasquitos Ranch with its well-preserved ranch house, which is worth a stop. The trail varies from narrow tracks to fire roads, but if you continue in a southwesterly direction and remain in the canyon, you will not get lost. At the 1-mile signpost, take the Wagon Wheel Trail to the left, cross the stream, and turn right on the main fire road. At the 0.5-mile signpost, turn right on the single-track trail that leads back to the start.

SIGNIFICANT TRAIL LANDMARKS

45A. Trailhead just off Sorrento Valley Boulevard through a gate.

45B. Turn left onto fire road at first intersection.

45C. Intersection with trail to waterfall on left. Visit falls or continue straight ahead.

45D. Black Mountain Road. Return to the start the way you came.

46
Poway Lake Loop

Distance: 2.7 miles

Course geometry: Loop

Running time: 0.5–0.8 hour

Start altitude: 1,100 feet

Finish altitude: 1,100 feet

Elevation gain: 450 feet

Highest altitude: 1,100 feet

Difficulty: Easy

Water: At the start and finish

Area management: Lake Poway Recreation Area

Maps: Escondido (USGS)

Poway Lake is located in beautiful Lake Poway Recreation Area at the western foot of Mount Woodson. Sycamore trees and large rock outcroppings ring the lake. Chaparral and dense shrubs cover the surrounding hills. Anglers patiently fish from the shore and from small boats. The trail begins at the parking lot and you pass by the bottom of the dam as the trail follows the

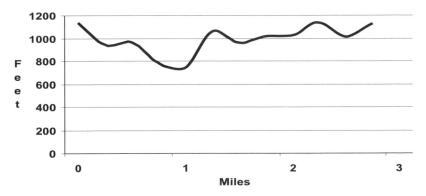

circumference of the lake on a 2.7-mile loop. Rolling hills lay to the north. For longer runs, there are trails leading to Lake Ramona or the top of Mount Woodson. Lake Poway is a great place for a family outing. The area includes picnic areas, a snack bar and bait shop, and restrooms. You can fish from shore or from boats rented at the lake. Swimming is not allowed.

GETTING THERE

Driving north on Interstate 15, exit at Poway Road and turn right (east). At Espola Road, turn left. At Lake Poway Road, turn right and drive to the park entrance. Parking is free. Driving south on Interstate 15, exit at Espola Road and turn left. Follow Espola Road first east and then south and turn left at Lake Poway Road.

Poway Lake

THE RUN

The trail begins at the northeast corner of the parking lot near the park office (46A). Follow the Poway Trail clockwise around the lake. It is clearly marked with small signs, but take notice of intersecting trails that lead to the left away from the lake. In 0.5 mile, you will descend to the base of the dam (46B). The Ramona Trail intersects on the left here.

Continue on the Poway Trail where rolling hills provide a good workout as the trail climbs a series of switchbacks back up above the dam. The vegetation consists of dense chaparral and heavy shrubs. At the south end of the lake, the Poway Trail intersects with the Mount Woodson trail (46C). Continue around the lake on the Poway Trail to return to the start.

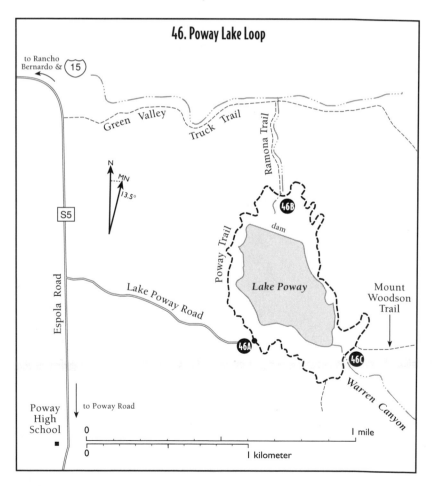

SIGNIFICANT TRAIL LANDMARKS

46A. Trailhead at northeast end of parking lot near park office.

46B. Base of the dam and intersection with Ramona Trail on left. Continue on Poway Trail.

46C. Intersection with the Mount Woodson Trail on the left. Continue on the Poway Trail.

47
Iron Mountain Summit Trail–Short Course

Distance: 6.4 miles

Course geometry: Out and back

Running time: 1–1.5 hours

Start altitude: 1,620 feet

Finish altitude: 1,620 feet

Elevation gain: 1,076 feet

Highest altitude: 2,696 feet

Difficulty: Moderate

Water: None

Area management: Lake Poway Recreation Area

Maps: San Vicente Reservoir (USGS)

This course is the most direct approach to the summit of Iron Mountain. The first 1.7 miles go to the base of Iron Mountain, and the next 1.5 miles climb to the summit on switchbacks. There are fantastic views in all directions, with hills south of the U.S. border clearly visible along with downtown San

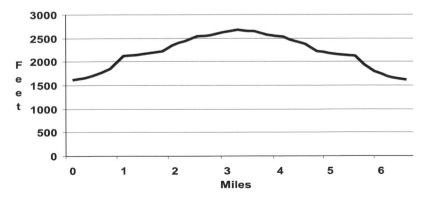

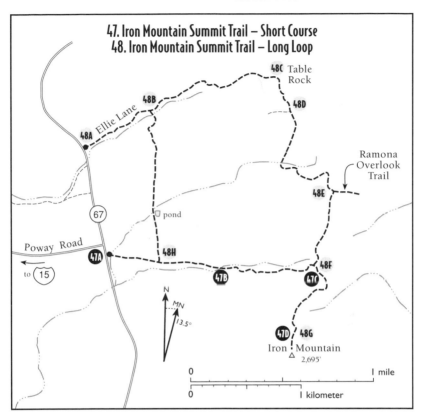

Diego and Point Loma. The landscape includes sage scrub, chaparral, and cactus growing amid large boulders and rock formations. The downhill return is exhilarating.

GETTING THERE

From San Diego, take Interstate 15 north to the Poway Road exit. Drive east (right) on Poway Road past Espola Road to Highway 67 and turn right. Park in the turnout just after turning right. Heading south on Interstate 15, exit at Carmel Valley Road and turn left. When you cross under the highway, Carmel Valley Road changes to Poway Road. Continue east on Poway Road to Highway 67 and turn right. Parking is free.

THE RUN

The trailhead is on the east side of Highway 67 (47A). From the trailhead,

Iron Mountain Summit Trail (Photo by Debbie Bradford)

head directly for Iron Mountain east across a relatively flat meadow. As you approach the hills, the trail begins to climb up a narrow canyon. Midway through the canyon, the trail crosses a streambed (47B).

At mile 1.7, a large sign on the right marks the right turn onto the Iron Mountain Peak Trail (74C). It is a 1.5-mile climb from here to the summit (47D). The lower sections of the approach to the summit are long, gently sloping switchbacks. Halfway up Iron Mountain, the trail follows the ridge and becomes somewhat steeper and rockier. The summit has spectacular views that are unforgettable. Record your thoughts in the logbook stored here after you capture the summit. Return to the start the way you came.

SIGNIFICANT TRAIL LANDMARKS
47A. Trailhead east of Highway 67.
47B. Streambed crossing.
47C. Right turn onto the Iron Mountain Peak Trail.
47D. Iron Mountain Peak summit. Return to the start the way you came.

48
Iron Mountain Summit Trail–Long Loop

Distance: 9.6 miles
Course geometry: Loop
Running time: 1.25–2.5 hours
Start altitude: 1,590 feet
Finish altitude: 1,590 feet
Elevation gain: 2,100 feet
Highest altitude: 2,696 feet
Difficulty: Strenuous
Water: None
Area management: Lake Poway Recreation Area
Maps: San Vicente Reservoir (USGS)

This course is the longer approach to the summit of Iron Mountain. The trail passes through coastal scrub, chaparral, and groves of eucalyptus and oak trees. Large granite boulders pepper the hillsides in stark contrast with the surrounding deep green foliage. Outstanding views of this beautiful area provide inspiration on the way to the summit.

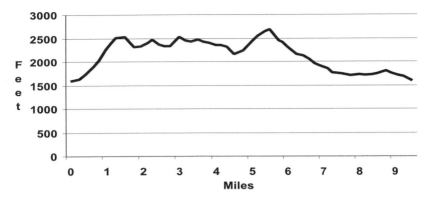

The final miles pass by a large pond in a grassy meadow, and the Iron Mountain summit is the run's climax. The beautiful rocks, greenery, and views of mountain ranges make this a glorious adventure.

GETTING THERE

From San Diego, take Interstate 15 north to the Poway Road exit. Drive east (right) on Poway Road past Espola Road to Highway 67 and turn left. Head 0.7 mile north to Ellie Lane; turn right and park in the parking lot.

Heading south on Interstate 15, exit at Carmel Valley Road and turn left (east). When you cross under the highway, Carmel Valley Road changes to Poway Road. Continue east on Poway Road past Espola Road to Highway 67 and turn left. Head 0.7 mile north to Ellie Lane; turn right and park in the parking lot. Parking is free.

THE RUN

The trailhead (48A) is on the northeast end of the parking area near a bulletin board. Follow the Ellie Lane Trail along the side of a large corral. At the end of the fence turn left onto the Iron Mountain Trail (48B). The trail on the right will be part of your return route later. The trail begins to climb a wide canyon, which has huge white granite boulders covering one side. The trail climbs along short switchbacks amid large rock formations and sage scrub.

A large oak tree marks the top of the canyon where the trail goes over a rock face known as Table Rock (48C). Follow the trail downhill into the next canyon. From here, you can see the trail continuing on the hillside to the east. Watch carefully for a false trail on the right (48D), and stay on the main trail to the left heading east. Next, a bend in the trail leads to the right, taking you around the side of a hill before the trail again turns eastward.

Iron Mountain Summit Trail

Continue up long switchbacks to a saddle. The excellent views from here include the vast Ramona Valley and distant mountains. Looking down the hillside you can see the Ramona Overlook Trail intersecting with the Iron Mountain Trail. Descend through this dry area to the intersection with the Ramona Overlook Trail (48E) on the left at mile 2.8. If time permits, run up this short trail for a better view of the Ramona Valley. Return to the Iron Mountain Trail and turn left. Iron Mountain is visible directly south.

The winding trail goes along a dry streambed at the base of the hills. Climb up a short hill to the start of the Iron Mountain Summit Trail (48F) marked by a large sign on the left. Take this trail 1.5 miles to the summit, elevation 2,696 feet. It goes up rocky switchbacks with a gentle grade. The slopes are rather barren, allowing you to see for many miles as you climb.

Once you've captured the summit (48G), you can record your impressions in the register and enjoy the feelings inspired by your achievement. Return down the summit trail to the intersection with the Iron Mountain Trail and turn left. This trail follows a shallow streambed west all the way to Highway 67. In advance of the highway, you will turn right onto the narrow continuation of the Iron Mountain Trail (48H) that you noted from the other end (48B) on the way in.

In this final section, you will go by a beautiful, reed-filled pond. Follow the trail on the left side of the pond and continue past the large corral to the intersection with Ellie Lane. Turn left and return to the start.

SIGNIFICANT TRAIL LANDMARKS

48A. Trailhead at northeast end of parking area.

48B. Intersection with the Iron Mountain Trail. Turn left onto trail.

48C. Table Rock. Large oak tree marks top of canyon.

48D. False trail leads right. Continue left on main trail.

48E. Intersection with the Ramona Overlook Trail. Run up trail if desired, otherwise continue straight ahead on Iron Mountain Trail.

48F. Intersection with the Iron Mountain Summit Trail. Turn left onto trail.

48G. Iron Mountain summit. Retrace steps to the Iron Mountain Trail and turn left onto trail.

48H. Turn right onto narrow trail, a continuation of the Iron Mountain Trail, just before reaching Highway 67. At intersection with Ellie Lane, turn left to return to start.

49
Cowles Mountain

Distance: 3 miles
Course geometry: Point to point
Running time: 0.5–1.25 hours
Start altitude: 650 feet
Finish altitude: 700 feet
Elevation gain: 950 feet
Highest altitude: 1,590 feet
Difficulty: Moderate
Water: At the start
Area management: Mission Trails Regional Park
Maps: La Mesa (USGS)

If you are looking for a quad-blasting experience on a short, steep climb, this is it. Cowles Mountain is the tallest mountain in the heart of San Diego. You will gain 950 feet in 1.5 miles on a challenging trail that is marked at quarter-mile

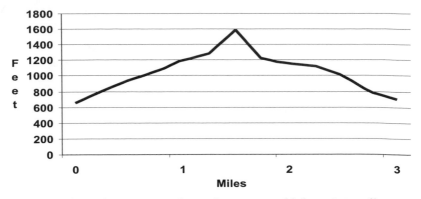

intervals. The trail is quite popular with runners and hikers. It is well-maintained, with wooden steps in the steeper areas and occasional solid-rock crossings. The trailhead has restrooms and water, and there are several fast-food restaurants nearby. Parking is free.

Due to the popularity of Cowles Mountain Trail, park rangers are particularly concerned about trail erosion, so stay on the trail at all times. Be courteous and pay close attention to other trail users, and always put safety first when passing.

GETTING THERE

From San Diego, drive east on Mission Valley Freeway (Interstate 8), exit on College Avenue, and turn left (north). Continue to Navajo Road and turn right. Pass the intersection with Golfcrest Drive (Cowles Mountain is visible on your left) and turn left onto Cowles Mountain Boulevard. Turn left on Boulder Lake Avenue, then right on Barker Way. Look for the trail on the left side of the road. This is where the run finishes, so park one car here on Barker Way.

With the second car, return to the intersection of Navajo Road and Golfcrest Drive. Turn right and park in the parking lot or on the street.

THE RUN

A large wooden sign marks the trailhead (49A) at the southeast end of the parking lot. The trail leads up Cowles Mountain on a series of switchbacks. The trail has trail markers every quarter-mile, making it convenient for interval training. At mile 0.9, the Barker Trail (49B) intersects on the right. Continue to the left.

After 1.5 miles you will reach the summit (49C), elevation 1,590 feet. Enjoy the sweeping views of the surrounding area. From the summit monument, head north on a fire road that soon turns toward the east. Halfway down, the Barker Trail (49D) again intersects on the right. Ignore this trail and continue straight ahead. After a wide bend to the right and just before reaching Barker Way, another trail (49E) intersects on the right. Do not take it. The run ends (49F) at a fence on Barker Way.

Option: If two cars are not available, make this an out-and-back run starting from either end. Alternatively, instead of taking the fire road to the summit, explore the intersecting trails at points 49B, 49D, and 49E. From the summit, another trail leads to Pyles Peak 2 miles to the northwest.

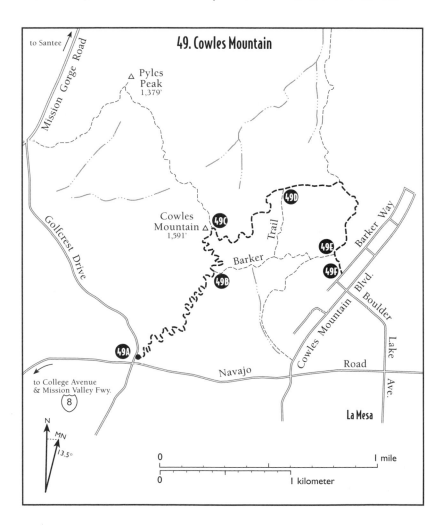

SIGNIFICANT TRAIL LANDMARKS

49A. Trailhead at southeast end of parking lot next to sign.

49B. Intersection with the Barker Trail on the right. Continue left.

49C. Cowles Mountain summit. Continue downhill on fire road just north of summit.

49D. Second intersection with the Barker Trail on the right. Continue straight ahead.

49E. Intersection with trail on the right. Ignore it.

49F. End of run at Barker Way.

Cowles Mountain

50
Noble Canyon

Distance: 10 miles
Course geometry: Point to point
Running time: 1.5–3 hours
Start altitude: 5,375 feet
Finish altitude: 3,715 feet
Elevation gain: 750 feet
Highest altitude: 5,500 feet
Difficulty: Strenuous
Water: None
Area management: Cleveland National Forest/DD
Maps: Monument Peak, Mount Laguna, and Decanso (USGS)

This course is full of contrasting terrain. The runner passes through pine forests; woodlands of oak and ferns; grassy meadows; and dry, rocky canyons spotted with yucca and cactus. Tranquil streams gurgling along the course carve through the rock formations and provide a source of nourishment for wildlife. The mountain views overlook deep canyons and large rock formations; this and numerous water crossings make this run very enjoyable.

Although this course is primarily downhill, there are some good climbs at the beginning and in the last 2 miles. There is no water on this run, so be sure to carry plenty. Setting up the point-to-point run with two cars involves a lot of driving, but it is well worth the effort to be able to enjoy this unique course.

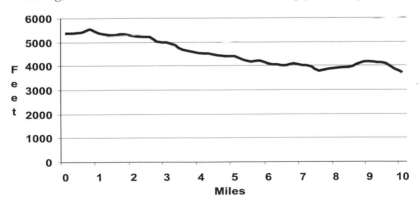

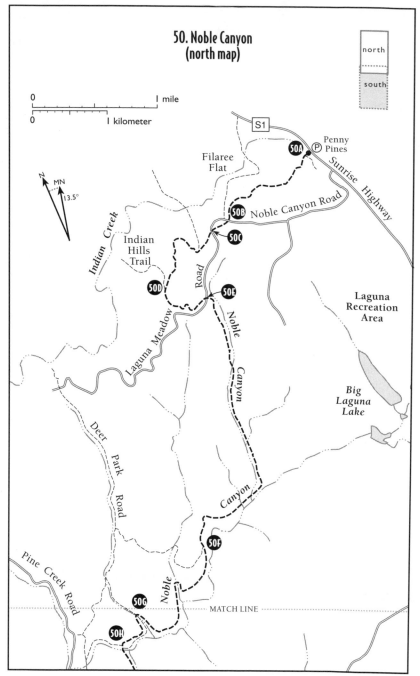

50. Noble Canyon
(north map)

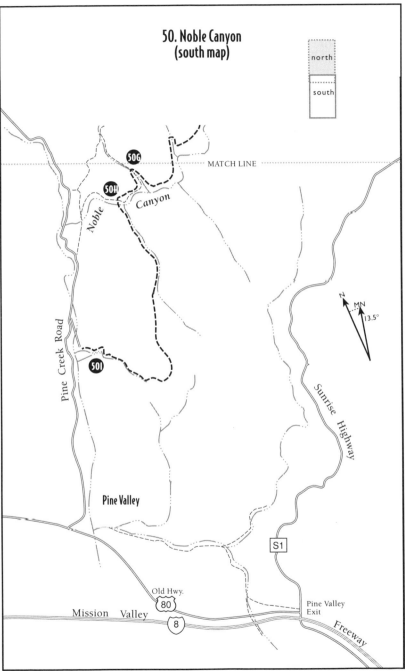

50. Noble Canyon
(south map)

north

south

50G

50H

MATCH LINE

Noble   Canyon

Pine Creek Road

50I

N

MN

13.5°

Sunrise Highway

Pine Valley

S1

Old Hwy.

80

Mission   Valley

8

Pine Valley
Exit

Freeway

Noble Canyon Trail

GETTING THERE

From San Diego, drive east on the Mission Valley Freeway (Interstate 8) to the Pine Valley turnoff. Turn left and drive 0.25 mile to Old Highway 80. Turn left and drive 1.2 miles to Pine Creek Road (just after the bridge) and turn right. Follow Pine Creek Road 1.6 miles to the trailhead turnoff (50I) and turn right. Watch your mileage closely as the road to the parking area is not well identified. Follow the road 0.25 mile to the end. This is where the run finishes, so leave one car here.

With the other car, return to Pine Creek Road and then Old Highway 80. Follow Old Highway 80 south and then east to the intersection with Sunrise Highway. Drive north on Sunrise Highway approximately 13 miles to the Penny Pines trailhead in the Laguna Mountains. Parking is available at the trailhead. Parking requires an Adventure Pass.

THE RUN

The trailhead (50A) is on the west side of Sunrise Highway across from the Penny Pines parking area. About 200 feet from the road, a secondary trail leads off to the left. Continue straight ahead on the Noble Canyon Trail as it begins to climb the side of a pine-covered hill. Fillafree Flat and the summit of Garnet Peak are visible from here.

At the bottom of a hill, the trail intersects with a road (50B). Pick up the trail directly across this road and continue west. Shortly after crossing the first road, another road (50C) intersects the trail near a cow gate. Cross over to the other side of the road and rejoin the trail to the right of the cow gate.

The trail descends and crosses a stream, then turns sharply to the right and goes up and around a short hill. After rounding the hill at mile 1.2, the Noble Canyon Trail is joined on the right by the Indian Hills Trail (50D). Continue straight ahead (west) on the main trail.

The trail crosses Noble Canyon Road (50E) and picks up again 50 feet to the right. Turn left and continue downhill.

You will soon reach the bottom of the canyon and a small stream in the deep shade of large oak trees. The trail becomes a rocky path in a steep, narrow gorge. When a small trail intersects on the right (50F) leading away from the canyon, continue straight on the Noble Canyon Trail. Follow the hillside as it skirts two shallow side canyons to where another trail on the right leads away from the canyon (50G). Continue on the main trail.

Just before the trail drops to a stream crossing, a sign marks another trail junction (50H). Take the left trail leading south down to the stream and into a grove of oak trees. The trail to the right leads back to Pine Creek Road.

Cross the stream and continue south, beginning a 2-mile climb through sage scrub and chaparral. After a brief climb to the saddle between two hills, the remainder is all downhill through some beautiful manzanita and laurel sumac to the finish (50I).

Option: If only one car is available, run out and back from either end of the run as far as desired.

SIGNIFICANT TRAIL LANDMARKS

50A. Trailhead on west side of Sunrise Highway.

50B. Intersection with a road. Pick up trail on opposite side.

50C. Intersection with a road. Pick up trail on opposite side to right of cow gate.

50D. Indian Hills Trail joins Noble Canyon Trail from the right. Continue straight ahead.

50E. Intersection with Noble Canyon Road. Pick up trail 50 feet to the right on opposite side and turn left.

50F. Intersection with small trail on the right in narrow gorge. Continue straight ahead.

50G. Intersection with trail on right leading away from the canyon. Continue straight ahead.

50H. Trail junction just before stream crossing. Go left and continue south across stream to grove of oak trees.

50I. Finish at Pine Creek Road parking area.

APPENDIXES

List of Trails

Distances are in miles, elevations are in feet, and running times are in hours. Run types are out and back (OB), loop (L), point to point (PTP), and out-and-back loop (OBL) combinations.

Run	Type	Mileage	Gain	High	Start	Finish	Time (hr)	Difficulty
1. Jesusita Trail	OB	8	2,400	1,830	500	500	1.3–2.3	Strenuous
2. Inspiration Point	OB	3.6	1,200	1,800	950	950	0.5–1	Strenuous
3. Rattlesnake Canyon	OB	3.5	1,050	1,880	940	940	0.5–1	Moderate
4. West Cold Springs Trail	OB	3.5	1,300	1,950	750	750	0.5–1	Strenuous
5. East Cold Springs Trail	OB	9	2,800	3,415	750	750	1.5–3	Strenuous
6. San Ysidro	OB	8.5	3,100	3,460	440	440	1.25–2.5	Strenuous
7. Romero Canyon	OB	13.5	2,500	3,100	925	925	1.75–3.25	Strenuous
8. Ray Miller Trail	L	10.7	1,500	1,050	50	50	1.5–3	Moderate
9. Sycamore Canyon to La Jolla Valley Loop	OBL	11.75	1,675	1,100	70	70	1.75–3.25	Moderate
10. Sycamore Canyon Loop	OBL	12	750	775	70	70	1.5–3	Moderate
11. Circle X Ranch to Sycamore Canyon	PTP	12	1,200	3,111	2,030	70	1.75–3.25	Strenuous
12. Latigo Canyon to Tapia Park	PTP	11.5	1,400	2,320	2,075	480	1.5–3	Moderate

Run	Type	Mileage	Gain	High	Start	Finish	Time (hr)	Difficulty
13. Tapia Park to Century Reservoir	OB	6	900	770	480	480	1–1.5	Easy
14. Malibu Creek State Park to Paramount Ranch	OB	8	1,200	930	600	600	1.25–2	Easy
15. Saddle Peak to Tapia Park	PTP	7.25	650	2,600	2,330	480	1–1.75	Easy
16. The Secret Trail	PTP	12	1,750	2,150	1,460	480	1.75–3.5	Moderate
17. Hondo Canyon	PTP	6	(1,500)	2,440	2,360	870	1–1.75	Easy
18. Santa Ynez Canyon to Michael Lane	L	9.5	1,400	2,104	600	600	1.5–2.3	Moderate
19. Santa Ynez Canyon to Will Rogers State Historic Park	PTP	11.25	1,500	2,104	600	420	1.5–3	Moderate
20. Santa Ynez Canyon to Los Liones Canyon	PTP	7.6	1,800	1,575	600	200	1.25–2	Moderate
21. Palisades Highlands to Trippet Ranch Loop	OBL	13.1	2,200	2,070	1,570	1,550	1.75–3.25	Strenuous
22. Palisades Highlands to Garapito Loop	OBL	11.5	1,800	2,070	1,570	1,570	1.75–3	Moderate
23. Palisades Highlands to Will Rogers State Historic Park	PTP	9.4	600	2,070	1,570	420	1.25–2.5	Moderate
24. Temescal Canyon Loop	L	3.5	1,160	1,160	300	300	0.5–1	Easy
25. Westridge to Temescal Canyon	PTP	13.75	1,700	2,040	1,260	300	2–3.5	Moderate

Run	Type	Mileage	Gain	High	Start	Finish	Time (hr)	Difficulty
26. Sullivan Canyon	OB	8.2	920	1,550	700	700	1.25–2	Moderate
27. Westridge to Mulholland Loop	OBL	14	1,900	1,960	1,260	1,260	2–3.5	Moderate
28. Catalina/Avalon Loop	L	8.6	900	1,510	730	10	1.5–2.5	Moderate
29. Franklin Canyon Loop	L	5.5	1,400	1,100	830	830	0.75–1.5	Easy
30. Griffith Park to Mount Hollywood	OBL	5.25	1,200	1,625	630	630	0.7–1.5	Easy
31. Cheeseboro Canyon	OBL	12.5	1,200	2,075	1,050	1,050	1.75–3.5	Moderate
32. Old Stagecoach Road	OB	4	1,050	1,800	1,000	1,000	0.75–1.25	Easy
33. Rocky Peak Trail	OB	7	1,200	2,714	1,575	1,575	1.25–2.5	Moderate
34. Placerita Canyon	OB	8.5	1,640	3,166	1,525	1,525	1.1–2.2	Moderate
35. Haines Canyon to Mount Lukens	OB	11.5	3,100	5,050	2,160	2,160	1.5–3	Moderate
36. Strawberry Peak	PTP	10.2	1,900	5,300	4,580	3,670	2–3.5	Strenuous
37. Santa Anita Canyon/ Upper Winter Creek Loop	L	8	2,340	3,612	2,170	2,170	1.25–2.5	Moderate
38. Shortcut Canyon	OB	8.8	1,700	4,700	4,700	4,700	1.5–3	Strenuous
39. Chilao Flat	OB	6.5	1,000	6,000	5,300	5,300	1.1–1.7	Moderate
40. Cooper Canyon	OB	13.6	2,818	7,000	7,000	7,000	2.3–3.4	Strenuous
41. Boy Scout Trail	OB	15.6	1,570	4,160	2,840	2,840	2.5–4.5	Moderate
42. Aliso and Wood Canyon Wilderness Park	OBL	8.5	1,800	1,010	1,010	1,010	1.25–2.5	Moderate

Run	Type	Mileage	Gain	High	Start	Finish	Time (hr)	Difficulty
43. El Moro Canyon	L	9	1,300	1,000	125	125	1.5–2.5	Moderate
44. Torrey Pines State Reserve	L	4.5	570	340	45	45	0.75–1.5	Easy
45. Los Peñasquitos Canyon Preserve	OB	12.5	450	300	65	65	1.75–2.5	Easy
46. Poway Lake Loop	L	2.7	450	1,100	1,100	1,100	0.5–0.8	Easy
47. Iron Mountain Summit Trail—Short Course	OB	6.4	1,076	2,696	1,620	1,620	1–1.5	Moderate
48. Iron Mountain Summit Trail—Long Loop	L	9.6	2,100	2,696	1,590	1,590	1.25–2.5	Strenuous
49. Cowles Mountain	PTP	3	950	1,590	650	700	0.5–1.25	Moderate
50. Noble Canyon	PTP	10	750	5,500	5,375	3,715	1.5–3	Strenuous

Management Resources

Angeles National Forest Headquarters
818-574-1613

California Department of Parks and Recreation
818-880-0350

Catalina Island Conservancy
310-510-2595

Cleveland National Forest
619-445-6235

Crystal Cove State Park
949-497-7648

Griffith Park, LA City Park Ranger
323-913-4688

Joshua Tree National Park
760-367-5520

Laguna Harbor and Parks
714-834-2400

Lake Poway Recreation Area
619-679-5465

Los Padres National Forest
805-967-3481

Los Peñasquitos Canyon Preserve
619-533-4067

Mission Trail Regional Park
619-668-3276

Mountain Parks Information
800-533-7276

Mountains Recreation and Conservation Authority
310-589-3230

Mountains Restoration Trust
818-346-9675

National Park Service
818-597-9192

Pueblo Lands of Santa Barbara
805-568-2460

Rancho Simi Recreation and Parks District
805-584-4400

Santa Monica Mountain Conservancy
   310-589-3200
Santa Monica Mountains National Recreation Area
   818-597-9192
Torrey Pines State Reserve
   619-755-2063

Responsible Trail Running Guidelines

These guidelines were written by Tom Sobal and first appeared in *Trail Times*, the newsletter published by the All American Trail Running Association (AATRA), Volume 3, No. 11. Tom Sobal and the AATRA have graciously allowed them to be reprinted here with minor modifications by the authors.

1. Stay on marked and existing trails.
2. Do not cut switchbacks.
3. Go through puddles, not around them.
4. Climb under or jump over fallen trees instead of going around them.
5. When multiple trails exist, run on the one that is the most worn.
6. Do not litter, leave no trace, and pack everything out that you packed in.
7. Use minimum impact techniques to dispose of human waste.
8. Leave what you find—take only photographs.
9. Close all gates that you open.
10. Stop to help others in need even while racing. Sacrifice your event to aid other trail users that might be in trouble.
11. Volunteer at trail races—before, after, and during the event.
12. Volunteer, support, and encourage others to participate in trail maintenance days.
13. Do not disturb or harass wildlife or livestock.
14. Stay off closed trails and obey all posted regulations.
15. Respect private property. Get permission first to go on private land.
16. Do not run on muddy or very dusty trails. Pick another route so that you do not damage the trail and cause unnecessary erosion.
17. Avoid startling other runners and trail users when passing from behind by calling out "hello" well in advance.
18. Know the area where you plan to run and let at least one other person know where you are going.

19. Dress for the conditions—both existing and potential.
20. Carry plenty of water.
21. Be ready to yield to other trail users (cyclists, hikers, and horses).
22. Uphill runners yield to downhill runners.
23. Know your limits.

BIBLIOGRAPHY

Bradford, Angier. *How to Stay Alive in the Woods.* New York: Collier Books, 1972.

Ford, Ray. *A Hiker's Guide to the Santa Barbara Front Country.* Santa Barbara County Recreational Map Series. Map No. 2. Santa Barbara, Calif.: McNally & Loftin Publishers, 1986.

Foster, Lynne. *Adventuring in the California Desert: The Sierra Club Travel Guide to the Great Basin, Mojave, and Colorado Desert Regions of California.* San Francisco: Sierra Club Books, 1987.

Hackett, M.D., Peter H. *Mountain Sickness Prevention, Recognition, and Treatment.* New York: The American Alpine Club, 1992.

Harrison, Tom. *Trail Map of the Angeles Front Country.* San Rafael, Calif.: Tom Harrison Cartography, 1992.

Harrison, Tom. *Trail Map of the Angeles High Country.* San Rafael, Calif.: Tom Harrison Cartography, 1990.

Harrison, Tom. *Trail Map of the San Diego Backcountry.* San Rafael, Calif.: Tom Harrison Cartography, 1997.

Harrison, Tom. *Trail Map of the San Gabriel Mountains.* San Rafael, Calif.: Tom Harrison Cartography, 1993.

Harrison, Tom. *Trail Map of the San Gorgonio Wilderness.* San Rafael, Calif.: Tom Harrison Cartography, 1996.

Harrison, Tom. *Trail Map of the San Jacinto Wilderness.* San Rafael, Calif.: Tom Harrison Cartography, 1995.

Harrison, Tom. *Trail Map of the Santa Monica Mountains Central.* San Rafael, Calif.: Tom Harrison Cartography, 1993.

Harrison, Tom. *Trail Map of the Santa Monica Mountains East.* San Rafael, Calif.: Tom Harrison Cartography, 1993.

Harrison, Tom. *Trail Map of the Santa Monica Mountains West.* San Rafael, Calif.: Tom Harrison Cartography, 1993.

McAuley, Milt. *Guide to the Backbone Trail of the Santa Monica Mountains.* Canoga Park, Calif.: Canyon Publishing Co., 1990.

McAuley, Milt. *Hiking Trails of the Santa Monica Mountains.* Canoga Park, Calif.: Canyon Publishing Co., 1980.

McAuley, Milt. *Wildflowers of the Santa Monica Mountains.* Canoga Park, Calif.: Canyon Publishing Co., 1996.

Robinson, John W. *Trail Map for San Bernardino Mountain Trails.* 4th ed. Berkeley, Calif.: Wilderness Press, 1997.

Robinson, John W. *Trail Map for Trail of the Angeles.* Berkeley, Calif.: Wilderness Press, 1989.

Schoenherr, Allan A. *A Natural History of California.* Berkeley and Los Angeles, Calif.: University of California Press, 1995.

Sharp, Robert P. *Geology Field Guide to Southern California.* Dubuque, Iowa: Kendal/Hunt Publishing Co., 1975.

Wheelock, Walt. *Southern California Peaks.* Glendale, Calif.: La Siesta Press, 1973.

INDEX

ABOUT THE AUTHORS

Stan Swartz founded the Trail Runners Club in 1988 and has been its director since inception. He also co-founded the Pacific Palisades Pacers Running Club before turning to trail running. He has organized many off-road running events and was invited to be an advisor to the All American Trail Running Association (AATRA).

Jim Wolff is an active outdoorsman and runner, as well as a marathoner. He is an active member of the Trail Runners Club of Santa Monica and former editor and publisher of the Trail Runners Club newsletter. He currently maintains the club's website. His articles have appeared in *UltraRunning* magazine.

Samir Shahin, M.D., is an avid runner and triathlete, completing 28 marathons and two Ironman triathlons in the past five years. He is the medical director of Expresscare Medical Clinic and the inventor of Sportslick skin lubricant. He is an accomplished pilot and a photographer.

From left, Jim Wolff, Stan Swartz, Samir Shahin, M.D. (Photo by Anthony Nex)

THE MOUNTAINEERS, founded in 1906, is a nonprofit outdoor activity and conservation club, whose mission is "to explore, study, preserve, and enjoy the natural beauty of the outdoors . . . . " Based in Seattle, Washington, the club is now the third-largest such organization in the United States, with 15,000 members and five branches throughout Washington State.

The Mountaineers sponsors both classes and year-round outdoor activities in the Pacific Northwest, which include hiking, mountain climbing, ski-touring, snowshoeing, bicycling, camping, kayaking and canoeing, nature study, sailing, and adventure travel. The club's conservation division supports environmental causes through educational activities, sponsoring legislation, and presenting informational programs. All club activities are led by skilled, experienced volunteers, who are dedicated to promoting safe and responsible enjoyment and preservation of the outdoors.

If you would like to participate in these organized outdoor activities or the club's programs, consider a membership in The Mountaineers. For information and an application, write or call The Mountaineers, Club Headquarters, 300 Third Avenue West, Seattle, WA 98119; 206-284-6310.

The Mountaineers Books, an active, nonprofit publishing program of the club, produces guidebooks, instructional texts, historical works, natural history guides, and works on environmental conservation. All books produced by The Mountaineers are aimed at fulfilling the club's mission.

Send or call for our catalog of more than 300 outdoor titles:

The Mountaineers Books
1001 SW Klickitat Way, Suite 201
Seattle, WA 98134
1-800-553-4453
mbooks@mountaineers.org
www.mountaineersbooks.org

TRAIL RUNNER, *The Magazine of Running Adventure,* is the first nationally distributed, full-color magazine devoted to off-road running. It covers all aspects of trail running, from leisurely fitness runs to grueling, high-altitude ultra-marathons, as well as snowshoeing, adventure racing, and orienteering. Our mission is to inform, entertain, and invigorate trail runners of all abilities with interesting news coverage, useful training and nutritional advice, critical product reviews, and inspirational features. *Trail Runner* is published in Boulder, Colo., by North South Publications, which also produces the award-winning climbing magazine *Rock & Ice.*

To subscribe, call toll-free 877-762-5423 or visit us online at www.trail runnermag.com.

Other titles you may enjoy from The Mountaineers:

100 HIKES IN™ SERIES: These are some of our fully detailed, best-selling hiking guides with complete descriptions, maps, and photos. Chock-full of trail data, safety tips, and wilderness etiquette.
100 HIKES IN™ CALIFORNIA'S CENTRAL SIERRA & COAST RANGE
100 HIKES IN™ NORTHERN CALIFORNIA

CONDITIONING FOR OUTDOOR FITNESS: A Comprehensive Training Guide, *David Musnick, M.D., and Mark Pierce, A.T.C.*
The most comprehensive guide to conditioning, fitness, and training for all outdoor activities. Chapters on specific sports, including hiking, climbing, biking, paddling, and skiing, with information on cross-training.

THE HIGH SIERRA: Peaks, Passes, and Trails, 2nd Edition, *R.J. Secor*
A new edition of the only guide to detail all the known routes on 570 peaks in the Sierras. This is the most comprehensive resource on this explorer's paradise and details all the major and minor routes in the area.

BICYCLING THE PACIFIC COAST: A Complete Route Guide, Canada to Mexico, 3rd Edition, *Tom Kirkendall and Vicky Spring*
Complete road guide for trip planning and touring along the entire Pacific Coast. Everything is included: from tunnel-riding strategies to where to get that flat fixed to the best side trips.

CLIMBING CALIFORNIA'S FOURTEENERS: 183 ROUTES TO THE FIFTEEN HIGHEST PEAKS, *Stephen F. Porcella and Cameron M. Burns*
This is the only guide covering multiple routes on each of California's fourteeners. Includes a general history of the mountains and historical anecdotes about the routes, with commentary from John Muir, Norman Clyde, and Clarence King.

EXTREME ALPINISM: Climbing Light, Fast, and High, *Mark F. Twight and James Martin*
A full-color master class on extreme alpine climbing by one of the world's elite mountaineers. Delivers an expert dose of reality and practical techniques for advanced climbers.